stitch style

Hats

First published in the UK in 2009 by
Collins & Brown
10 Southcombe Street
London
W14 0RA

An imprint of Anova Books Company Ltd

Distributed in the United States and Canada by
Sterling Publishing Co, 387 Park Avenue South,
New York, NY 10016-8810, USA

ISBN 978-1-84340-486-6

A CIP catalogue for this book is available from
the British Library.

10 9 8 7 6 5 4 3 2 1

Photography by Rebecca Maynes
Illustrations by Kang Chen

Reproduction by Rival Colour Ltd, UK
Printed and bound by NPE Print Communication
Pte Ltd, Singapore

This book can be ordered direct from the
publisher. Contact the marketing department, but
try your bookshop first.

www.anovabooks.com

stitchstyle

20 Fashion Knit and Crochet Styles

Hats

COLLINS & BROWN

Introduction

With **Stitch Style Hats**, the **Stitch Style** strand of books brings you another fabulous collection of fashion-following knitted and crocheted accessories. Whatever the hat style you love – maybe a slouchy beret, a cool cap or a beaded beanie – there's something here for you to make. Designed by and for style-concious knitters everywhere, there are hats in fabulous cashmere yarns and warm wools so you can look good on the chilliest winter days.

If you are a novice knitter, then start with a simple beanie hat knitted in chunky yarn on big, straight needles, so it'll grow quickly. There are patterns for texture lovers and designs for colour queens, so plenty to choose from whatever your knitting and crochet skill level.

Every project has full pattern instructions and there are lots of tips that will make your knitting easier, plus ideas for customising designs so they fit perfectly into your unique wardrobe. If you are unsure of a technique, turn to the back of the book for some how-tos that will help.

Contents

DESIGNED BY

Carol Meldrum

Lattice beanie

Knitted with three ends of yarn on big, straight needles, this little hat will knit up in a flash. The subtle colour changes are created by using two different-coloured yarns and they complement the textured stitch pattern beautifully.

YARN

Rowan *Cocoon* (80% merino wool, 20% kid mohair), approx. 100g (3½oz)/115m (125yd) per ball

   2 balls of Scree 803 (A)

   1 ball of Alpine 802 (E)

NEEDLES

Pair of 10.00mm (US 15) knitting needles

TENSION (GAUGE)

9 sts and 12 rows = 10cm (4in) square measured over St st using 10.00mm (US 15) needles and 3 strands of yarn held together

TO FIT

One size

SKILL LEVEL

Intermediate

HAT

With two strands of A and one strand of B held together (3 strands in total), cast on 41 sts.

Row 1 (RS): K1, *p1, k1; rep from * to end.

Row 2: P1, *k1, p1; rep from * to end.

Row 3: *P1, k1, yfwd, skpo, p1, k1, p1, k2, p1, m1; rep from * to last st, k1 (45 sts).

Row 4: K1, *k2, [p1, k1] twice, p2tog tbl, yrn, p2, k1; rep from * to end.

Row 5: *[P1, k1] twice, yfwd, skpo, p1, k2, p2, m1; rep from * to last st, p1 (49 sts).

Row 6: K1, *k3, p1, k1, p2tog tbl, yrn, p1, k1, p2, k1; rep from * to end.

Row 7: *[P1, k1] 3 times, yfwd, skpo, k1, p3, m1; rep from * to last st, p1 (53 sts).

Row 8: K1, *k4, p2tog tbl, yrn, [p1, k1] twice, p2, k1; rep from * to end.

Row 9: *P1, k1, yfwd, skpo, p1, k1, p1, k2, p4; rep from * to last st, p1.

Row 10: K1, *k4, [p1, k1] twice, p2tog tbl, yrn, p2, k1; rep from * to end.

Row 11: *[P1, k1] twice, yfwd, skpo, p1, k2, p4; rep from * to last st, p1.

Row 12: K1, *k4, p1, k1, p2tog tbl, yrn, p1, k1, p2, k1; rep from * to end.

Row 13: *[P1, k1] 3 times, yfwd, skpo, k1, p4; rep from * to last st, p1.

Row 14: K1, *k4, p2tog tbl, yrn, [p1, k1] twice, p2, k1; rep from * to end.

Rows 15–18: As rows 9–12.

Row 19: *[P1, k1] 3 times, yfwd, skpo, k1, p2, p2tog; rep from * to last st, p1 (49 sts).

Row 20: K1, *k3, p2tog tbl, yrn, [p1, k1] twice, p2, k1; rep from * to end.

Row 21: *P1, k1, yfwd, skpo, p1, k1, p1, k2, p1, p2tog; rep from * to last st, p1 (45 sts).

Row 22: K1, *k2, [p1, k1] twice, p2tog tbl, yrn, p2, k1; rep from * to end.

Row 23: *[P1, k1] twice, yfwd, skpo, p1, k2, p2tog; rep from * to last st, p1 (41 sts).

Row 24: *K2tog, p1, k1, p2tog tbl, yrn, p1, k1, p2; rep from * to last st, k1 (37 sts).

Row 25: *K2tog, [p1, k1] twice, yfwd, skpo, k1; rep from * to last st, p1 (33 sts).

Row 26: K1, *p2tog tbl, yrn, [p1, k1] twice, p2; rep from * to end.

Row 27: *[K1, p1] twice, k1, k3tog; rep from * to last st, k1 (25 sts).

Row 28: P1, *p3tog, k1, p1, k1; rep from * to end.

Break off yarn and thread through rem 17 sts. Pull up tight and fasten off securely.

FINISHING

Sew in all loose ends. Do NOT press. Sew back seam using mattress stitch.

TIP

If you find the three ends of yarn tricky to handle, you can wind up one big ball made up of all three yarns before you start the knitting.

DESIGNED BY

Claire Garland

Tweedy cloche

Sweet and neat, this crochet cloche is worked in a felted yarn that is soft and easy to wear. The contrast brim adds a vivid colour accent, which is echoed in the simple bead detailing on the front.

YARN

Rowan *Felted Tweed* (50% merino wool, 25% alpaca, 25% viscose), approx. 50g (1¾oz)/175m (191yd) per ball

    1 ball of Ginger 154 (A)

Rowan *Pure Wool DK* (100% superwash wool), approx. 50g (1¾oz)/125m (136yd) per ball

    1 ball of Tea Rose 025 (B)

NEEDLES

5.50mm (I/9) crochet hook

6.00mm (J/10) crochet hook

EXTRAS

Two 15mm (⅝in) clear pink faceted glass beads

TENSION (GAUGE)

8 sts and 9 rows = 10cm (4in) square measured over dc (sc) fabric using 6.00mm (J/10) hook and two strands of A held together

TO FIT

One size

SKILL LEVEL

Intermediate

CLOCHE

With 6.00mm (J/10) hook and two strands of A held together, make 3 ch and join with a ss (sl st) to form a ring.

Round 1: 1 ch (does NOT count as st), 9 dc (sc) into ring, ss (sl st) to first dc (sc) (9 sts).

Round 2: 1 ch (does NOT count as st), 2 dc (sc) into each dc (sc) to end, ss (sl st) to first dc (sc) (18 sts).

Round 3: 1 ch (does NOT count as st), *1 dc (sc) into next dc (sc), 2 dc (sc) into next dc (sc); rep from * to end, ss (sl st) to first dc (sc) (27 sts).

Round 4: 1 ch (does NOT count as st), *1 dc (sc) into each of next 2 dc (sc), 2 dc (sc) into next dc (sc); rep from * to end, ss (sl st) to first dc (sc) (36 sts).

Round 5: 1 ch (does NOT count as st), *1 dc (sc) into each of next 3 dc (sc), 2 dc (sc) into next dc (sc); rep from * to end, ss (sl st) to first dc (sc) (45 sts).

Round 6: 1 ch (does NOT count as st), *1 dc (sc) into each of next 4 dc (sc), 2 dc (sc) into next dc (sc); rep from * to end, ss (sl st) to first dc (sc) (54 sts).

Round 7: 1 ch (does NOT count as st), *1 dc (sc) into each of next 8 dc (sc), 2 dc (sc) into next dc (sc); rep from * to end, ss (sl st) to first dc (sc) (60 sts).

Round 8: 1 ch (does NOT count as st), *1 dc (sc) into each of next 9 dc (sc), 2 dc (sc) into next dc (sc); rep from * to end, ss (sl st) to first dc (sc) (66 sts).

Round 9: 1 ch (does NOT count as st), 1 dc (sc) into each dc (sc) to end, ss (sl st) to first dc (sc).

Rounds 10–15: As round 9.

Round 16: 1 ch (does NOT count as st), *1 dc (sc) into each of next 10 dc (sc), miss next dc (sc); rep from * to end, ss (sl st) to first dc (sc) (60 sts).

Round 17: As round 9.

Round 18: 1 ch (does NOT count as st), *1 dc (sc) into each of next 9 dc (sc), miss next dc (sc); rep from * to end, ss (sl st) to first dc (sc) (54 sts).

Round 19: As round 9.

Round 20: 1 ch (does NOT count as st), *1 dc (sc) into each of next 8 dc (sc), miss next dc (sc); rep from * to end, ss (sl st) to first dc (sc) (48 sts).

Round 21: As round 9.

Cut off A and join in B.

Change to 5.50mm (I/9) crochet hook.

Round 22: 1 ch (does NOT count as st), 2 dc (sc) into each dc (sc) to end, ss (sl st) to first dc (sc) (96 sts).

Rounds 23–26: As round 9.

Fasten off.

FINISHING

Sew in all loose ends, block and press.
Attach beads as in photograph.

TIP

As the brim of the cloche will frame your face, work it in a yarn colour to complement your skin tone. If you are dark-skinned, then the bright pink shown will be perfect. For an olive skin, consider a turquoise or lilac colour. If you are pale-skinned, then a fresh green or a soft grey will look great.

DESIGNED BY

Fair Isle beret

Working traditional Fair Isle patterns in contemporary colours gives them a fresh twist that fits in perfectly with today's vintage fashions. This is also a great hat for bad-hair days, as it's big enough to tuck away frizzy curls and bed-head locks.

YARN

Rowan *Pure Wool DK* (100% superwash wool), approx.

50g (1¾oz)/125m (136yd) per ball

  1 ball of Hay 014 (A)

  1 ball of Barley 015 (B)

  1 ball of Avocado 019 (C)

  1 ball of Shale 002 (D)

  1 ball of Damson 030 (E)

  1 ball of Kiss 036 (F)

  1 ball of Glade 021 (G)

NEEDLES

Pair of 3.25mm (US 3) knitting needles

Pair of 4.00mm (US 6) knitting needles

TENSION (GAUGE)

24 sts and 32 rows = 10cm (4in) square measured over patt using 4.00mm (US 6) needles

TO FIT

One size

SKILL LEVEL

Intermediate

BERET

Using 3.25mm (US 3) needles and A, cast on 108 sts.

Row 1 (RS): *K1, p1; rep from * to end.

Row 2: As row 1.

These 2 rows form rib.

Cont in rib for 7 rows more, ending with a RS row.

Row 10 (WS): Rib 1, m1, rib 1, *m1, rib 2; rep from * to end (162 sts).

Change to 4.00mm (US 6) needles.

Repeating the 8-st patt rep 20 times across each row and working first and last sts as indicated, work in St st from chart as follows:

Work chart rows 1–18, ending with a WS row.

Row 19 (RS): With A, k1, *m1, k8; rep from * to last st, k1 (182 sts).

Row 20: *With E p1, with A p1; rep from * to end.

Row 21: *With E k1, with A k1; rep from * to end.

Row 22: With A, purl.

Row 23: With A, k1, *skpo, k7; rep from * to last st, k1 (162 sts).

Work chart rows 24 – 28.

Row 29 (RS): With A, k1, *skpo, k8; rep from * to last st, k1 (146 sts).

Row 30: With A, purl.

Repeating the 8-st patt rep 18 times across each row and working first and last sts as indicated, work in St st from chart as follows:

Work chart rows 1 and 2, ending with a WS row.

Row 33 (RS): With A, k1, *skpo, k7; rep from * to last st, k1 (130 sts).

Now repeating the 8-st patt rep 16 times across each row and working first and last sts as indicated, work in St st from chart as follows:

Work chart rows 4 – 16, ending with a WS row.

Row 47 (RS): With A k1, with G k1, *with A skpo, k1, with G k1; rep from * to end (98 sts).

Row 48: With A, purl.

Row 49: With A, k1, *skpo; rep from * to last st, k1 (50 sts).

Rows 50–51: As rows 20–21.

Row 52: With A, p1, *p2tog tbl; rep from * to last st, p1 (26 sts).

Row 53: As row 49.

Break off yarn and thread through rem 14 sts. Pull up tight and fasten off securely.

FINISHING

Sew in all loose ends, block and press. Join back seam.

TIP

For a striking, graphic look, you could work this beret with a white background and replace the colours with black and shades of grey and slate blue. To do this you'll almost definitely have to use yarns from different ranges to get the right colours, and this is fine as long as the tension (gauge) of each is similar. Collect together all the yarns you want to use and check that the average tensions (gauges) given on the ball bands are all similar, both to each other and to the project tension (gauge) – a stitch or row different either way is fine. Knit a tension (gauge) swatch in the Fair Isle pattern and measure it carefully before you start your hat.

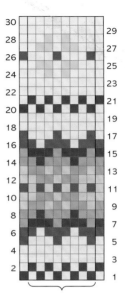

Key

▢	Hay 014 (A)
▨	Barley 015 (B)
▦	Avocado 019 (C)
▨	Shale 002 (D)
◼	Damson 030 (E)
◼	Kiss 036 (F)
◼	Glade 021 (G)

DESIGNED BY

Elizabethan beret

Classic colours and historical inspiration combine to make a deliciously pretty beret that'll look perfect at any event, be it a winter wedding or summer party. Team it with a white wool coat or black and white floral print dress.

YARN

Rowan Classic *Cashcotton DK* (35% cotton, 25% polyamide, 18% angora, 13% viscose, 9% cashmere), approx. 50g (1¾oz)/130m (142yd) per ball

  1 ball of White 600 (A)
  1 ball of Black 607 (B)

NEEDLES

Set of four 3.25mm (US 3) double-pointed needles
Set of four 4.00mm (US 6) double-pointed needles
3.25mm (D/3) crochet hook

EXTRAS

75cm (29½in) of 7-cm (2¾-in) wide black lace
One 6-mm (¼-in) diameter silver pearl bead

TENSION (GAUGE)

22 sts and 30 rows = 10cm (4in) square measured over St st using 4.00mm (US 6) needles

TO FIT

One size

SKILL LEVEL

Intermediate

BERET

Using 3.25mm (US 3) needles and B, cast on 120 sts. Divide sts evenly across three dpns; join for working in the round.

Rounds 1–8: *K2, p2; rep from * to end.

Round 9: *Rib 4, inc in next st; rep from * to end (144 sts).

Cut off B and join in A.

Rounds 10–36: Knit.

Round 37: K2tog, k15, *sl 1, k2tog, psso, k15; rep from * to last st, slip last st and then pass this slipped st over first st of round (at beg of next round) (128 sts).

Rounds 38–39: Knit.

Round 40: K2tog, k13, *sl 1, k2tog, psso, k13; rep from * to last st, slip last st and then pass this slipped st over first st of round (at beg of next round) (112 sts).

Rounds 41–42: Knit.

Round 43: K2tog, k11, *sl 1, k2tog, psso, k11; rep from * to last st, slip last st and then pass this slipped st over first st of round (at beg of next round) (96 sts).

Rounds 44–45: Knit.

Round 46: K2tog, k9, *sl 1, k2tog, psso, k9; rep from * to last st, slip last st and then pass this slipped st over first st of round (at beg of next round) (80 sts).

Rounds 47–48: Knit.

Round 49: K2tog, k7, *sl 1, k2tog, psso, k7; rep from * to last st, slip last st and then pass this slipped st over first st of round (at beg of next round) (64 sts).

Rounds 50–51: Knit.

Round 52: K2tog, k5, *sl 1, k2tog, psso, k5; rep from * to last st, slip last st and then pass this slipped st over first st of round (at beg of next round) (48 sts).

Round 53: Knit.

Round 54: K2tog, k3, *sl 1, k2tog, psso, k3; rep from * to last st, slip last st and then pass this slipped st over first st of round (at beg of next round) (32 sts).

Round 55: Knit.

Round 56: K2tog, k1, *sl 1, k2tog, psso, k1; rep from * to last st, slip last st and then pass this slipped st over first st of round (at beg of next round) (16 sts).

Rounds 57–58: Knit.

Break off yarn and thread through rem 16 sts. Pull up tight and fasten off securely.

FLOWER

With B, make 6 ch and join with a ss (sl st) to form a ring.

Round 1: 1 ch (does NOT count as st), 1 dc (sc) into ring, *(1 tr (dc), 1 dtr (tr), 4 ch and 1 dc (sc)) into ring; rep from * 5 times more, replacing dc (sc) at end of last rep with ss (sl st) to first dc (sc) (6 petals).

Round 2: [4 ch (keeping this ch behind petals of prev round), 1 ss (sl st) into next dc (sc)] 6 times, working last ss (sl st) into same place as ss (sl st) at end of prev round.

Round 3: 1 ch (does NOT count as st), (1 dc (sc), 1 tr (dc), 1 dtr (tr), 4 ch, 1 dc (sc), 1 tr (dc), 1 dtr (tr), 4 ch and 1 dc (sc)) into each ch sp to end, ss (sl st) to first dc (sc) (12 petals).

Round 4: [5 ch (keeping this ch behind petals of prev round), miss 1 dc (sc), 1 ss (sl st) into next dc (sc)] 6 times, working last ss (sl st) into same place as ss (sl st) at end of prev round.

Cut off B and join in A.

Round 5: 1 ch (does NOT count as st), (1 dc (sc), 8 ch, 1 dc (sc) and 8 dc (sc)) into each ch sp to end, replacing '8 ch' at end of last rep with '4 ch, 1 tr (dc) into first dc (sc)' (12 ch sps).

Round 6: 3 ch (counts as first tr (dc)), 1 tr (dc) into ch sp partly formed by tr (dc) at end of prev round, *4 ch**, (2 tr (dc), 2 ch and 2 tr (dc)) into next ch sp; rep from * to end, ending last rep at **, 2 tr (dc) into same ch sp as used at beg of round, 2 ch, ss to top of 3 ch at beg of round.

Round 7: 1 ch (does NOT count as st), 1 dc (sc) into st at base of 1 ch, 1 dc (sc) into next tr (dc), *(2 dc (sc), 6 ch and 2 dc (sc)) into next ch sp, 1 dc (sc)

into each of next 2 tr (dc), 2 dc (sc) into next ch sp**, 1 dc (sc) into each of next 2 tr (dc); rep from * to end, ending last rep at **, ss to first dc (sc).

Fasten off.

FINISHING

Sew in all loose ends, block and press. Join ends of lace. Using photograph as a guide, neatly sew lace to Beret, positioning lace just above rib section in B – ensure lace is sewn on so that Beret will still stretch enough to fit onto head. Attach Flower to Beret as in photograph, attaching the pearl bead in the centre.

> ### TIP
>
> This beret would also look fabulous knitted in a strong colour, such a deep turquoise, and trimmed with cotton lace in a lighter shade of the same colour. As yarn is available in such a wide range of colours and lace in a smaller range, it may be best to pick the lace first and then find a yarn to go with it.

DESIGNED BY

Be seen beret

This pillbox-style beret is a real scene-stealer. Worked in the finest cashmere yarn on slender needles, it isn't the quickest hat to make, but the end result is worth every second of work.

YARN

Jade Sapphire *2-ply Mongolian cashmere* (100% pure cashmere), approx. 55g (2oz)/365m (399yd) per skein

   1 skein of Cousin Coral 058

NEEDLES

Set of four 2.00mm (US 0) double-pointed needles

EXTRAS

Small amount of waste yarn (for cast on)

Eight stitch markers

TENSION (GAUGE)

36 sts and 52 rows = 10cm (4in) square measured over patt using 2.00mm (US 0) needles

TO FIT

One size

SKILL LEVEL

Advanced

SPECIAL ABBREVIATIONS

See page 95 for information on MK.

BERET

With waste yarn, cast on 208 sts. Divide sts evenly across three dpns; join for working in the round.

Round 1: Knit.

Cut off waste yarn and join in main yarn.

Now work crown section as follows:

Round 1: [K26, PM] 8 times.

Round 2: [Knit to within 2 sts of M, k2tog, SM to RH needle] 8 times (200 sts).

Round 3: [Knit to marker, SM to RH needle] 8 times.

Working MK at random over St st sections, rep last 2 rounds 24 times more.

Break off yarn and thread through rem 8 sts. Pull up tight and fasten off securely.

LOWER SECTION

Carefully unravel waste yarn at cast on edge and slip the 208 sts of first round in main yarn onto dpns.

Join in main yarn and, working downwards from crown section, cont as follows:

Round 1: P1, knit to end.

Round 2: Purl.

Round 3: As round 1.

Round 4: [P24, p2tog] 8 times (200 sts).

Round 5: Knit to end, winding yarn round needle twice for each st.

Round 6: *Slip next 4 sts onto RH needle, dropping extra loops, slip same 4 sts back onto LH needle, p4tog leaving sts on LH needle, now work (k1, p1, k1) into same 4 sts and let all 4 sts fall from LH needle; rep from * to end.

Rounds 7–9: As rounds 1–3.

Round 10: [P23, p2tog] 8 times (192 sts).

Rounds 11–12: As rounds 5 and 6.

Rounds 13–15: As rounds 1–3.

Round 16: [P22, p2tog] 8 times (184 sts).

Rounds 17–18: As rounds 5 and 6.

Rounds 19–22: As rounds 1 and 2, twice.

Rounds 23–30: *K1, p1; rep from * to end.

Cast (bind) off in rib.

FINISHING

Sew in all loose ends, block and press.

TIP

You could knit this hat in a fine crochet yarn, which is available in many colours including some fantastic metallics. Do work a tension (gauge) swatch and check the stitch and row counts carefully before you start the project or you may discover that after all that work your new hat really doesn't fit. A little tassel made as for the one on the Beaded Beret (page 76) could be sewn to the top of this beret as a finishing touch.

DESIGNED BY

Claire Garland

Beaded cap

A retro classic, this perky cap is knitted in a chunky yarn that really makes the most of the textured stitch pattern. The vivid pinks of the base and peak are picked up in the line of stitched-on beads.

YARN

Rowan *Scottish Tweed Chunky* (100% pure new wool), approx. 100g (3½oz)/100m (109yd) per ball

   1 ball of Olive Green 035 (A)

Rowan *Pure Wool DK* (100% superwash wool), approx. 50g (1¾oz)/125m (136yd) per ball

   1 ball of Tea Rose 025 (B)

   1 ball of Pomegranate 029 (C)

NEEDLES

Pair of 4.00mm (US 6) knitting needles

Pair of 4.50mm (US 7) knitting needles

Pair of 7.00mm (US 10½) knitting needles

4.50mm (G/6) crochet hook

EXTRAS

Six 6-mm (¼-in) diameter pink pearl beads

TENSION (GAUGE)

10 sts and 12 rows = 10cm (4in) square measured over moss (seed) st using 7.00mm (US 10½) needles and A

TO FIT

One size

SKILL LEVEL

Intermediate

CAP

Using 4.50mm (US 7) needles and two strands of B held together, cast on 76 sts.

Row 1 (RS): *K2, p2; rep from * to end.

Rows 2–7: As row 1.

Cut off B and join in A.

Row 8 (WS): Purl.

Row 9: *K1, p1; rep from * to end.

Row 10: *P1, k1; rep from * to end.

Last 2 rows form moss (seed) st.

Cont in moss (seed) st until Hat measures 4cm (1½in) from cast on edge, ending with a WS row.

SHAPE CROWN

Row 1 (RS): [Moss (seed) st 16 sts, work 3 tog] 4 times (68 sts).

Work 3 rows.

Row 5: [Moss (seed) st 14 sts, work 3 tog] 4 times (60 sts).

Work 3 rows.

Row 9: [Moss (seed) st 3 sts, work 3 tog] 10 times (40 sts).

Work 1 row.

Row 11: [Moss (seed) st 1 st, work 3 tog] 10 times (20 sts).

Work 5 rows.

Row 17: [Work 2 tog] 10 times.

Work 1 row.

Break off yarn and thread through rem 10 sts. Pull up tight and fasten off securely.

PEAK

Using 4.00mm (US 6) needles and C, cast on 36 sts.

Starting with a purl row, work in St st for 9 rows, ending with a WS row.

Row 10 (RS): Skpo, knit to last 2 sts, k2tog.

Row 11: P2tog, purl to last 2 sts, p2tog tbl.

Working all decreases as set by last 2 rows, dec 1 st at each end of next 6 rows (20 sts).

Row 18 (RS): Skpo, k8 and turn, leaving rem 10 sts on a holder.

Work on this set of 9 sts only for first section.

Dec 1 st at end of next row, then at both ends of foll row.

Rep last 2 rows once more (3 sts).

Row 25 (WS): P1, p2tog.

Row 26: K2tog and fasten off.

Return to sts left on holder and rejoin C with RS facing.

Row 18 (RS): K to last 2 sts, k2tog (9 sts).

Dec 1 st at beg of next row, then at both ends of foll row.

Rep last 2 rows once more (3 sts).

Row 25 (WS): P2tog tbl, p1.

Row 26: K2tog and fasten off.

FINISHING

Sew in all loose ends. Do NOT press. Sew up back seam of Cap using mattress stitch.

Sew centre seam of Peak for last 6 rows. Fold Peak so that shaped row-end edges match cast on edge and sew open edges together. Positioning Peak at centre front of Cap, sew joined Peak edges to cast on edge of rib section in B.

Using photograph as a guide, sew beads onto main section of Cap in a line from centre of Peak to top of crown.

With 4.50mm (G/6) crochet hook and two strands of B held together, make 12 ch and fasten off. Form strip into a loop and attach to top of Cap as in photograph.

DESIGNED BY

Sue Bradley

Lace snood

The perfect combination of pretty and practical, this snood will keep you cosy and looking good. Make it a permanent fixture in your handbag during the winter months and whip it out when the wind blows.

YARN

Rowan *Damask* (57% viscose, 22% linen, 21% acrylic), approx. 50g (1¾oz)/105m (114yd) per ball

  2 balls of Mica 040

NEEDLES

Pair of 3.75mm (US 5) knitting needles

TENSION (GAUGE)

24 sts and 29 rows = 10cm (4in) square measured over St st using 3.75mm (US 5) needles

TO FIT

One size

SKILL LEVEL

Intermediate

SNOOD

Cast on 123 sts.

Row 1 (RS): K1, *p1, k1; rep from * to end.

Row 2: P1, *k1, p1; rep from * to end.

These 2 rows form rib.

Cont in rib until work measures 14cm (5½in), ending with a WS row.

Next row (RS): K1, p1, *k3tog, [p1, k1] twice, p1; rep from * to last st, k1 (93 sts).

Cont in rib until work measures 16cm (6¼in), ending with a WS row.

Cast (bind) off 14 sts at beg of next 2 rows (65 sts).

Now work in lace patt as follows:

Row 1 (RS): P2, *k5, p2; rep from * to end.

Row 2: K2, *p5, k2; rep from * to end.

Row 3: P2, *k2tog, yfwd, k1, yfwd, skpo, p2; rep from * to end.

Row 4: As row 2.

These 4 rows form lace patt.

Cont in lace patt until work measures 27cm (10½in) **from cast on edge**, ending with a WS row.

Keeping patt correct, cast (bind) off 16 sts at beg of next 2 rows (33 sts).

Cont straight in patt until work measures 10cm (4in) from cast (bound) off sts, ending with a WS row.

Cut yarn and leave rem 33 sts on a holder.

Sew row-end edges of last 10cm (4in) to cast (bound) off sts.

BORDER

With RS facing and 3.75mm (US 5) needles, pick up and knit 14 sts along first cast (bound) off edge of rib section, and 22 sts up row-end edge, patt across 33 sts on holder, pick up and knit 22 sts down other row-end edge, then 14 sts along other cast (bound) off edge (105 sts).

Starting with row 2, work in rib as given for lower edge for 11 rows, ending with a WS row.

Cast (bind) off in rib.

FINISHING

Sew in all loose ends, block and press. Sew centre front chin seam using mattress stitch.

DESIGNED BY

Tweed cap

Making the most of self-striping yarn, this cap also uses a stitch-weaving pattern that makes for a firm knitted fabric so the cap holds its shape. Wear your cap with skinny jeans and an over-sized, chunky jumper or a long leather coat.

YARN

Twilleys *Freedom Spirit* (100% pure new wool), approx. 50g (1¾oz)/120m (131yd) per ball

3 balls of Essence 507 (A)

Twilleys *Freedom Wool* (100% pure new wool), approx. 50g (1¾oz)/50m (54yd) per ball

1 ball of Navy 423 (B)

NEEDLES

Pair of 6.50mm (US 10½) knitting needles

Set of four 6.50mm (US 10½) double-pointed needles

3.75mm (F/5) crochet hook

EXTRAS

Piece of buckram 12cm (4¾in) by 30cm (11¾in)

One 25-mm (1-in) diameter self-cover button

70cm (27½in) of 12-mm (½-in) wide satin ribbon

Matching sewing thread

TENSION (GAUGE)

25 sts and 34 rows = 10cm (4in) square measured over patt using 6.50mm (US 10½) needles and A

TO FIT

One size

SKILL LEVEL

Intermediate

CROWN PANELS (MAKE 6)

Using 6.50mm (US 10½) needles and A, cast on 25 sts.

Row 1 (RS): K1, *bring yarn to front (RS) of work, slip next st purlwise, take yarn to back (WS) of work, k1; rep from * to end.

Row 2: Sl 1, *p1, take yarn to back (RS) of work, slip next st purlwise, bring yarn to front (WS) of work; rep from * to end.

These 2 rows form patt.

Cont in patt, inc 1 st at each end of next and 2 foll 8th rows, taking inc sts into patt (31 sts).

Work 9 rows, ending with a WS row.

Keeping patt correct, dec 1 st at each end of next and 4 foll 4th rows, then on foll 9 alt rows, ending with a RS row.

Next row (WS): P3tog and fasten off.

BAND AND PEAK

Matching fasten-off points of all six sections at centre of crown, sew Crown Panels together along row-end edges, leaving cast on edges free.

Starting at one seam, using 6.50mm (US 10½) dpns, A and with RS facing, pick up and knit 143 sts around cast on edge of Crown Panels (this is 24 sts for the first five sections and 23 sts for the sixth section). Divide sts evenly across three dpns and work in rounds as follows:

Round 1: K1, *bring yarn to front (RS) of work, slip next st purlwise, take yarn to back (WS) of work, k1; rep from * to end.

Round 2: *Bring yarn to front (RS) of work, slip next st purlwise, take yarn to back (WS) of work, k1; rep from * to last st, bring yarn to front (RS) of work, slip next st purlwise, take yarn to back (WS) of work.

These 2 rounds form patt.

Work 5 rounds more – band section completed.

SHAPE PEAK

**Keeping patt correct (by working patt as given for Crown Panels) and working backwards and forwards in short rows, shape peak as follows:

Rows 1–2: Patt 2 sts, turn.

Row 3 (RS): Patt 4 sts, turn.

Row 4: Patt 2 sts, turn.

Rows 5–6: Patt 6 sts, turn.

Row 7: Skpo, patt 6 sts, turn.

Row 8: Patt 8 sts, turn.

Rows 9–10: Patt 9 sts, turn.

Row 11: Skpo, patt 9 sts, turn.

Row 12: Patt 10 sts, turn.

Rows 13–14: Patt 13 sts, turn.

Row 15: Skpo, patt 14 sts, turn.

Row 16: Patt 15 sts, turn.

Row 17: Skpo, patt 21 sts, turn.

Row 18: Patt 22 sts, turn.

Row 19: Skpo, patt 66 sts, turn.

Rows 20–21: As rows 1–2.

Rows 22–23: As row 3.

Row 24: Patt 6 sts, turn.

Row 25: Patt 4 sts, k2tog, turn.

Rows 26–27: Patt 7 sts, turn.

Rows 28–29: Patt 9 sts, turn.

Rows 30–31: Patt 10 sts, turn.

Row 32: Patt 13 sts, turn.

Row 33: Patt 11 sts, k2tog, turn.

Row 34: Patt 15 sts, turn.

Row 35: Patt 13 sts, k2tog, turn.

Row 36: Patt 22 sts, turn.

Row 37: Patt 20 sts, k2tog, turn.

Row 38: Patt 62 sts, turn.

Now working on these 62 sts only (in rows), complete peak as follows:

Row 39 (RS): Skpo, patt to last 2 sts, k2tog (60 sts).

Row 40: Patt to end.

Row 41: Skpo, patt to last 2 sts, k2tog.

Row 42: P2tog, patt to last 2 sts, p2tog tbl.

Rows 43–46: As rows 41–42, twice (48 sts).

Row 47: sl 1, k2tog, psso, patt to last 3 sts, k3tog.

Row 48: P3tog, patt to last 3 sts, p3tog tbl.

Rows 49–54: As rows 47–48, 3 times. Cast (bind) off rem 16 sts.

PEAK LINING

Using 6.50mm (US 10½) needles and
A, cast on 72 sts.

Row 1 (WS): Sl 1, *p1, take yarn to
back (RS) of work, slip next st purlwise,
bring yarn to front (WS) of work; rep
from * to end.

This row sets position of patt as given
for Crown Panels.

Complete as given for Band and Peak
from ** to end.

PEAK TRIM

Using 6.50mm (US 10½) double-
pointed needles and B, cast on 3 sts.

Row 1: K3, *without turning work slip
these 3 sts to opposite end of needle
and bring yarn to opposite end of work
pulling it quite tightly across WS of
work, now knit these 3 sts again; rep
from * until Trim measures 29cm
(11½in).

Cast (bind) off.

BUTTON COVER

Using 6.50mm (US 10½) needles and
A, cast on 2 sts.

Row 1 (RS): Inc once in each st (4 sts).

Row 2: Inc in first st, p2, inc in last st
(6 sts).

Row 3: Inc in first st, [k1, bring yarn to
front (RS) of work, slip next st purlwise,
take yarn to back (WS) of work] twice,
inc in last st (8 sts).

Row 4: [P1, take yarn to back (RS) of
work, slip next st purlwise, bring yarn to
front (WS) of work] 4 times.

Row 5: [K1, bring yarn to front (RS) of
work, slip next st purlwise, take yarn to
back (WS) of work] 4 times.

Row 6: As row 4.

Row 7: Skpo, [k1, bring yarn to front
(RS) of work, slip next st purlwise, take
yarn to back (WS) of work] twice, k2tog
(6 sts).

Row 8: P2tog, take yarn to back (RS) of
work, slip next st purlwise, bring yarn to
front (WS) of work, p1, p2tog tbl (4 sts).

Row 9: Skpo, k2tog (2 sts).

Row 10: P2tog and fasten off.

FINISHING

Sew in all loose ends, block and press
the pieces.

Trim buckram to same size as Peak
Lining section and tack in place to WS
of Peak Lining. Matching edges of Peak
and Peak Lining, pin and tack Peak
Lining in place, sandwiching buckram
between knitted layers. Using 3.75mm
(F/5) crochet hook and A, work a round
of dc (sc) around lower edge of Band
and Peak, working sts around edge of
Peak through Peak Lining as well (to join
sections) and ending with ss to first dc
(sc). Fasten off. Slip stitch cast on edge
of Peak Lining in place on inside.

Sew Peak Trim around Band along top
edge of Peak.

Following manufacturers instructions,
cover button with Button Cover, then
attach to top of Cap.

Trim ribbon to fit neatly around inside of
Band, allowing extra for seam. Join ends,
then neatly slip stitch ribbon in place to
inside of Band.

TIP

Before you sew the crown panels together, lay them out on a work surface and arrange them in a circle to best advantage. If you particularly like the stripe sequence on one panel, put that one at the front of the cap.

Sew together the row-ends of the crown panels using mattress stitch. To match the edges of the panels perfectly, lay one panel next to another and put a safety pin through both of the fasten-off points. Put another safety pin through the row-end edge of both pieces at the widest point of the section and a third pin through the row-end edges at the bottom, cast-on edge. Start sewing from the bottom edge.

Sew three pairs of panels together in this way. Then pin the three sections together in the same way as before and sew those seams.

DESIGNED BY

Gosia Dzik-Holden

Reversible cap

A soft, easy-to-wear cap with a contrast inner so you can team it with different outfits and always be brilliantly co-ordinated. Choose colours to match your wardrobe staples and it'll be the most useful hat you've ever owned.

YARN

Debbie Bliss *Cashmerino DK* (55% merino wool, 33% microfibre, 12% cashmere), approx. 50g (1¾oz)/110m (120yd) per ball

   1 ball of Red 04 (A)

Debbie Bliss *Pure Silk* (100% silk), approx. 50g (1¾oz)/125m (136yd) per skein

   1 skein of Turquoise 07 (B)

NEEDLES

Set of four 3.75mm (US 5) double-pointed needles

EXTRAS

Small amount of waste yarn (for cast on)

Eight stitch markers

TENSION (GAUGE)

24 sts and 35 rows = 10cm (4in) square measured over St st using 3.75mm (US 5) needles

TO FIT

One size

SKILL LEVEL

Advanced

SPECIAL NOTE

Cap is made in two identical sections. Make first section following instructions given below, then make second section in exactly the same way, but reversing position of colours by reading B for A, and vice versa.

CROWN

Using waste yarn, cast on 128 sts.
Divide sts evenly across three dpns; join
for working in the round.

Round 1: Knit.

Cut off waste yarn and join in A.

Round 2: Knit.

Rep this round until Crown measures
4.5cm (1¾in) from rounds in
waste yarn.

SHAPE CROWN

Now shape crown as follows:

Round 1: [K16, PM] 8 times.

Round 2: [K to within 2 sts of M,
k2tog, SM to RH needle] 8 times
(120 sts).

Round 3: [K to marker, SM to RH
needle] 8 times.

Rep last 2 rounds 12 times more
(24 sts).

Round 28: [K1, k2tog, SM to RH
needle] 8 times (16 sts).

Round 29: [K2tog, SM to RH needle]
8 times.

Break off yarn and thread through rem
8 sts. Pull up tight and fasten off securely.

LOWER SECTION

Carefully unravel waste yarn at cast on
edge of Crown and slip the 128 sts of
first round in A onto dpns.

Join in A and, working downwards from
crown section, cont as follows:

Round 1 (RS): K15, cast (bind) off next
26 sts, knit to end, then knit first 15 sts
of round again.

Now working backwards and forwards in
rows, not rounds, cont on these 102 sts
as follows:

Row 2 (WS): sl 1, p to end.

Row 3: sl 1, k3, k2tog, k to last 6 sts,
skpo, k4.

Rows 4–11: As rows 2–3, 4 times (92
sts).

Row 12: As row 2.

SHAPE LOWER EDGE

Row 1 (RS): sl 1, (p1, k1) into next st,
k1, skpo, turn.

**Row 2 and every foll alt row to row
30:** Slip first st on RH needle onto LH
needle rotating it by 180°, p2tog tbl,
p to end.

Row 3: sl 1, (p1, k1) into next st, k2,
skpo, turn.

Row 5: sl 1, (p1, k1) into next st, k3,
skpo, turn.

Row 7: sl 1, (p1, k1) into next st, k4,
skpo, turn.

Row 9: sl 1, (p1, k1) into next st, k5,
skpo, turn.

Row 11: sl 1, (p1, k1) into next st, k6,
skpo, turn.

Row 13: sl 1, (p1, k1) into next st, k7,
skpo, turn.

Row 15: sl 1, (p1, k1) into next st, k8,
skpo, turn.

Row 17: sl 1, (p1, k1) into next st, k9,
skpo, turn.

Row 19: sl 1, (p1, k1) into next st,
k10, skpo, turn.

Rows 21, 23, 25, 27–29: sl 1, k12,
skpo, turn.

**Row 30 and every foll alt row to
end:** Slip first st on RH needle onto LH
needle rotating it by 180°, p2tog tbl,
p to last 3 sts, p2tog, p1.

Row 31: sl 1, k2tog, k9, skpo, turn.

Row 33: sl 1, k2tog, k7, skpo, turn.

Row 35: sl 1, k2tog, k5, skpo, turn.

Row 37: sl 1, k2tog, k3, skpo, turn.

Row 39: sl 1, k2tog, k1, skpo, turn.

Row 40: Slip first st on RH needle onto
LH needle rotating it by 180°, p2tog tbl,
p2tog, p1.

Cut yarn.

With WS facing, rejoin yarn to rem
51 sts and work second half of lower
edge shaping as follows:

Row 1 (WS): sl 1, p2, p2tog, turn.

**Row 2 and every foll alt row to row
22:** Slip first st on RH needle onto LH
needle, k2tog, k to last 2 sts, (k1, p1)
into next st, k1.

Row 3: sl 1, p3, p2tog, turn.

Row 5: sl 1, p4, p2tog, turn.

Row 7: sl 1, p5, p2tog, turn.

Row 9: sl 1, p6, p2tog, turn.

Row 11: sl 1, p7, p2tog, turn.

Row 13: sl 1, p8, p2tog, turn.

Row 15: sl 1, p9, p2tog, turn.

Row 17: sl 1, p10, p2tog, turn.

Row 19: sl 1, p11, p2tog, turn.

Rows 21: sl 1, p12, p2tog, turn.

Row 22: Slip first st on RH needle onto LH needle, k2tog, k to end.

Rows 23–28: As rows 21–22, 3 times.

Row 29: As row 21.

Row 30 and every foll alt row to row 38: Slip first st on RH needle onto LH needle, k2tog, k to last 3 sts, skpo, k1.

Row 31: sl 1, p2tog tbl, p9, p2tog, turn.

Row 33: sl 1, p2tog tbl, p7, p2tog, turn.

Row 35: sl 1, p2tog tbl, p5, p2tog, turn.

Row 37: sl 1, p2tog tbl, p3, p2tog, turn.

Row 39: sl 1, p2tog tbl, p9, p2tog, turn.

Row 40: Slip first st on RH needle onto LH needle, k2tog, skpo, k1. Cast (bind) off rem 10 sts purlwise.

EMBROIDERY

With B, swiss darn square onto Cap following photograph – position square centrally over centre back 5 sts and approx. 4 rows down from final cast (bound) off edge.

FINISHING

Make second Cap section in exactly the same way, referring to note on page 43. Sew in all loose ends, block and press. Slip second Cap inside first Cap, with WS together and matching lower shaped edges. With B, join Caps by working a line of chain stitch (on RS of first section) very close to lower edge.

TIP

Using two different yarns for your cap is a great idea as you get a texture change as well as a colour change when you turn it inside out. However, do make sure that the yarns you choose knit up to the same tension (gauge), or one section of you cap could be bigger than the other section.

DESIGNED BY

Carol Meldrum

Winter warmer

Cosy earflaps and soft, fluffy yarn knitted up using two strands held together make this hat super-warm on the chilliest days. Whether you're a ski bunny or a street cyclist, this is a great winter hat.

YARN

Rowan *Kid Classic* (70% lambswool, 26% kid mohair, 4% nylon), approx. 50g (1¾oz)/140m (153yd) per ball

   1 ball of Nightly 846 (A)

   1 ball of Feather 828 (B)

Rowan *Felted Tweed* (50% merino wool, 25% alpaca, 25% viscose), approx. 50g (1¾oz)/175m (191yd) per ball

   1 ball of Rage 150 (C)

NEEDLES

Pair of 8.00mm (US 11) knitting needles

Cable needle

TENSION (GAUGE)

14 sts and 16 rows = 10cm (4in) square measured over St st using 8.00mm (US 11) needles and 2 strands of yarn held together

TO FIT

One size

SKILL LEVEL

Intermediate

EARFLAPS (MAKE 2)

With two strands of A held together, cast on 3 sts.

Row 1 (RS): K1, p1, k1.

Row 2: P1, k1, p1.

Rows 3–4: As rows 1–2.

Row 5: K1, m1, p1, m1, k1 (5 sts).

Row 6: P2, k1, p2.

Row 7: K1, m1, k1, p1, k1, m1, k1 (7 sts).

Row 8: P1, [k1, p1] 3 times.

Row 9: K1, m1, [p1, k1] twice, p1, m1, k1 (9 sts).

Row 10: P2, [k1, p1] 3 times, p1.

Row 11: K1, m1, [k1, p1] 3 times, k1, m1, k1 (11 sts).

Row 12: P1, [k1, p1] 5 times.

Row 13: K1, [p1, k1] 5 times.

Row 14: As row 12.

Row 15: K1, m1, [p1, k1] 4 times, p1, m1, k1 (13 sts).

Row 16: P2, [k1, p1] 5 times, p1.

Row 17: K2, [p1, k1] 5 times, k1.

Row 18: As row 16.

Row 19: K1, m1, [k1, p1] 5 times, k1, m1, k1 (15 sts).

Row 20: [P1, k1] 7 times, p1.

Row 21: [K1, p1] 7 times, k1.

Row 22: As row 20.

Cut off yarn and leave sts on a holder.

MAIN SECTION

With two strands of A held together, cast on 6 sts, turn and work across 15 sts of first Earflap as follows: [k1, p1] 7 times, k1, turn and cast on 21 sts, turn and work across 15 sts of second Earflap as follows: [k1, p1] 7 times, k1, turn and cast on 6 sts (63 sts).

Row 1 (WS): P1, *k1, p1; rep from * to end.

Row 2: K1, *p1, k1; rep from * to end.

Rows 3–4: As rows 1–2.

Row 5: As row 1.

Row 6 (RS): P2tog, [k1, p1] twice, *k7, [p1, k1] twice, p1; rep from * to last 9 sts, k7, p2tog (61 sts).

Row 7: K1, *p7, [k1, p1] twice, k1; rep from * to end.

Change to two strands of B held together.

Row 8: With B, *[p1, k1] twice, p1, k7; rep from * to last st, p1.

Row 9: As row 7 but with B.

Cut off B and cont using two strands of A held together.

Row 10: *[P1, k1] twice, p1, k7; rep from * to last st, p1.

Row 11: As row 7.

Row 12: As row 10.

Row 13: As row 7.

Row 14: *[P1, k1] twice, p1, slip next 3 sts onto cn and leave at front of work, k4, then k3 from cn; rep from * to last st, p1.

Row 15: As row 7.

Row 16: As row 10.

Row 17: As row 7.

Change to two strands of C held together.

Row 18: As row 8 but with C.

Row 19: As row 7 but with C.

Cut off C and cont using two strands of A held together.

Rows 20–25: As row 12–17.

Row 26: *P1, [k1, p1] twice, k3, skpo, k2; rep from * to last st, p1 (56 sts).

Row 27: K1, *p6, [k1, p1] twice, k1; rep from * to end.

Row 28: *P1, [k1, p1] twice, k6; rep from * to last st, p1.

Row 29: As row 27.

Change to two strands of B held together.

Row 30: With B, *p1, [k1, p1] twice, k2, skpo, k2; rep from * to last st, p1 (51 sts).

Row 31: With B, k1, *p5, k1, [p1, k1] twice; rep from * to end.

Cut off B and complete Hat using two strands of A held together.

Row 32: *P1, [k1, p1] twice, slip next 3 sts onto cn and leave at front of work, k2, then k3 from cn; rep from * to last st, p1.

Row 33: K1, *p5, k1, [p1, k1] twice; rep from * to end.

Row 34: *P1, [k1, p1] twice, k1, sl 1, k2tog, psso, k1; rep from * to last st, p1 (41 sts).

Row 35: K1, *p3, k1, [p1, k1] twice; rep from * to end.

Row 36: *P1, [k1, p1] twice, sl 1, k2tog, psso; rep from * to last st, p1 (31 sts).

Row 37: K1, *p1, k1; rep from * to end.

Row 38: P1, *k1, p1, k1, sl 1, k2tog, psso; rep from * to end (21 sts).

Row 39: *P2, k1, p1; rep from * to last st, k1.

Break off yarn and thread through rem 21 sts. Pull up tight and fasten off securely.

FINISHING

Sew in all loose ends. Do NOT press. Sew back seam using mattress stitch. With A, make two plaits, each 25cm (10in) long, and knot one end to form a tiny tassel. Attach other ends of plaits to cast on edges of Earflaps.

DESIGNED BY

Rib beanie

Chunky yarn, easy stripes and simple stitches mean that this is a great hat project for a novice knitter. When using the doubled yarn, just use one end from the outside and one end from the inside of the ball and treat them as though they were a single strand.

YARN

Rowan *Cocoon* (80% merino wool, 20% kid mohair), approx. 100g (3½oz)/115m (125yd) per ball

- 1 ball of Mountain 805 (A)
- 1 ball of Shale 804 (C)
- 1 ball of Alpine 802 (E)

Rowan *Little Big Wool* (67% wool, 33% nylon), approx. 50g (1¾oz)/60m (65yd) per ball

- 1 ball of Agate 511 (B)
- 1 ball of Topaz 509 (D)

NEEDLES

Pair of 8.00mm (US 11) knitting needles

TENSION (GAUGE)

13 sts and 20 rows = 10cm (4in) square measured over St st using 8.00mm (US 11) needles

TO FIT

One size

SKILL LEVEL

Beginner

SPECIAL NOTE

Use Rowan *Cocoon* **DOUBLE** throughout.

HAT

With A, cast on 62 sts.

Row 1 (RS): K2, *p2, k2; rep from * to end.

Row 2: P2, *k2, p2; rep from * to end. These 2 rows form rib.

Keeping rib correct and joining in and breaking off colours as required, now work in stripes as follows:

Rows 3–4: With B.

Rows 5–6: With C.

Rows 7–8: With D.

Rows 9–10: With E.

Rows 11–12: With B.

Rows 13–16: With A.

Rows 17–18: With D.

Rows 19–20: With C.

SHAPE CROWN

Row 21: With C, *[k2, p2] twice, k2, p2tog; rep from * to last 2 sts, k2 (57 sts).

Row 22: With C, p2, *k1, p2, [k2, p2] twice; rep from * to end.

Row 23: With B, *[k2, p2] twice, k2, p1; rep from * to last 2 sts, k2.

Row 24: With B, p2, *k1, p2, [k2, p2] twice; rep from * to end.

Row 25: With E, *[k2, p2] twice, k1, k2tog; rep from * to last 2 sts, k2 (52 sts).

Row 26: With E, *p4, k2, p2, k2; rep from * to last 2 sts, p2.

Row 27: With E, [k2, p2] twice, *k4, p2, k2, p2; rep from * to last 4 sts, k4.

Row 28: As row 26.

Row 29: With D, *[k2, p2] twice, k2tog; rep from * to last 2 sts, k2 (47 sts).

Row 30: With D, p3, *k2, p2, k2, p3; rep from * to last 8 sts, [k2, p2] twice.

Row 31: With A, k2, *p2, k2, p1, k3tog, k1; rep from * to end (37 sts).

Row 32: With A, p2, *k1, p2, k2, p2;

rep from * to end.

Row 33: With A, k2, *p2, k1, k3tog, k1; rep from * to end (27 sts).

Row 34: With A, *p3, k2; rep from * to last 2 sts, p2.

Row 35: With A, k2, *p1, k3tog, k1; rep from * to end (17 sts).

Row 36: With A, p2, *k1, p2; rep from * to end.

Break off yarn and thread through rem 17 sts. Pull up tight and fasten off securely.

FINISHING

Sew in all loose ends. Do NOT press. Sew back seam using mattress stitch, taking care to match up stripes.

TIP

This basic hat pattern can easily be customised without affecting the size or shape. You can knit it in a stripe sequence of your own invention, or in a plain colour, with maybe just a stripe or two around the bottom edge as a border.

DESIGNED BY

Fiona McTague

Inca hat

A palette of muted but clean and graphic colours takes away any hint of 'earth mother' that can otherwise creep in to this style of hat, and the perky pom-poms add a great finishing touch.

YARN

Rowan Classic *Baby Alpaca DK* (100% baby alpaca), approx. 50g (1¾oz)/100m (109yd) per ball

  2 balls of Jacob 205 (A)

  1 ball of Southdown 208 (B)

  1 ball of Lincoln 209 (C)

NEEDLES

Pair of 3.25mm (US 3) knitting needles

Pair of 3.75mm (US 5) knitting needles

3.25mm (US 3) circular knitting needle

TENSION (GAUGE)

24 sts and 36 rows = 10cm (4in) square measured over patt using 3.75mm (US 5) needles

TO FIT

One size

SKILL LEVEL

Advanced

EARFLAPS (MAKE 2)

Using 3.75mm (US 5) needles and A, cast on 9 sts.

Row 1 (WS): Purl.

Starting with a knit row, joining in and cutting off yarns as required and stranding yarn not in use loosely across WS of work, now work in St st from chart A as follows:

Inc 1 st at each end of next 5 rows, then on foll 5 alt rows, taking inc sts into patt (29 sts).

Cont straight until all 28 rows of chart A have been completed, ending with a WS row.

Cut yarn and leave sts on a holder.

MAIN SECTION

Using 3.75mm (US 5) needles and A, cast on 15 sts, turn and, with RS facing, knit across 29 sts of first Earflap, turn and cast on 33 sts, turn and, with RS facing, knit across 29 sts of second Earflap, turn and cast on 15 sts (121 sts).

Join in C.

Row 1 (WS): With A p1, *with C p1, with A p1; rep from * to end.

Row 2: With C k1, *with A k1, with C k1; rep from * to end.

Row 3: With A, purl.

Repeating the 20-st patt rep 6 times across each row and working edge st as indicated, work in St st from chart B until all 20 rows have been completed, ending with a WS row.

Row 24 (RS): With A, knit.

Row 25: With A, purl.

Row 26: With B, knit.

Row 27: As row 25.

Row 28: As row 2.

Row 29: As row 1.

Row 30: As row 24.

Row 31: With B, purl.

Row 32: As row 24.

Row 33: With C p1, *with A p3, with C p1; rep from * to end.

Row 34: With B k2, *with A k1, with B k3; rep from * to last 3 sts, with A k1, with B k2.

Row 35: As row 31.

SHAPE CROWN

Row 1 (RS): With A, [k10, k2tog] 10 times, k1 (111 sts).

Row 2: With B, purl.

Row 3: With A, knit.

Row 4: With C p1, *with A p1, with C p1; rep from * to end.

Row 5: With A k1, *with C k1, with A k1; rep from * to end.

Row 6: With A, p1, [p2tog, p9] 10 times (101 sts).

Row 7: With B, knit.

Row 8: With A, p1, [p2tog, p8] 10 times (91 sts).

Row 9: With C, knit.

Row 10: With A, p1, [p2tog, p7] 10 times (81 sts).

Row 11: With B, knit.

Row 12: With A, p1, [p2tog, p6] 10 times (71 sts).

Row 13: As row 5.

Row 14: As row 4.

Row 15: With A, knit.

Row 16: With B, purl.

Row 17: With A, [k5, k2tog] 10 times, k1 (61 sts).

Row 18: With C, purl.

Row 19: With A, [k4, k2tog] 10 times, k1 (51 sts).

Row 20: With B, purl.

Row 21: With A, [k3, k2tog] 10 times, k1 (41 sts).

Rows 22–23: As rows 4–5.

Row 24: With A, purl.

Row 25: With B, [k2, k2tog] 10 times, k1 (31 sts).

Row 26: With A, purl.

Row 27: With C, [k1, k2tog] 10 times, k1 (21 sts).

Row 28: With A, purl.

Row 29: With B, [k2tog] 10 times, k1. Break off yarn and thread through rem 11 sts. Pull up tight and fasten off securely.

Chart A

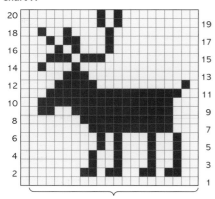

Key

☐ 2 balls of Jacob 205 (A)
■ 1 ball of Southdown 208 (B)
▨ 1 ball of Lincoln 209 (C)

Chart B

TIP

You could also knit this hat in a brights colour palette. Consider a strong aqua background with the Fair Isle worked in hot pink and tangerine, or a lime green background with turquoise and sea-blue patterning. Make the pom-poms in either the background colour, as here, or make the cords in one of the Fair Isle colours and the pom-poms in the other.

If you prefer, you can Swiss-darn the reindeers' antlers after you have finished the knitting. Many knitters find it tricky to work single stitches neatly in intarsia and Swiss darning them is a good alternative.

LOWER BORDER

Using 3.25mm (US 3) circular needle, with RS facing and A, pick up and knit across 15 sts from first cast on section of Main Section, 28 sts down row-end edge of first Earflap, 8 sts from cast on edge of this Earflap, 28 sts up other row-end edge of this Earflap, 33 sts from next cast on edge of Main Section, 28 sts down row-end edge of other Earflap, 8 sts from cast on edge of this Earflap, 28 sts up other row-end edge of this Earflap, then 15 sts from rem cast on section of Main Section (191 sts). Work in garter st for 4 rows, ending with a RS row.

Cast (bind) off knitwise (on WS).

FINISHING

Sew in all loose ends, block and press. Join back seam. With A, make two 5-cm (2-in) diameter pom-poms and two twisted cords, each 13cm (5in) long. Attach a pom-pom to one end of one cord, then attach other end of cord to lower edge of Earflap as in photograph. Attach other cord and pom-pom to other Earflap in same way.

Isle hat

Slouchy and easy-to-wear, this hat will look good if you have long or short hair, wayward curls or a sleek crop. Wear it pulled down, as here, or push it back on your forehead and let your fringe peep out.

YARN

Rowan *Scottish Tweed 4-ply* (100% pure new wool), approx. 25g (1oz)/110m (120yd) per ball

   4 balls of Oatmeal 025 (A)

   1 ball of Sea Green 006 (B)

   1 ball of Porridge 024 (C)

   1 ball of Peat 019 (D)

   1 ball of Rust 009 (E)

   1 ball of Gold 028 (F)

NEEDLES

Set of four 3.00mm (US 2) double-pointed needles
Set of four 3.25mm (US 3) double-pointed needles

TENSION (GAUGE)

28 sts and 38 rows = 10cm (4in) square measured over St st using 3.25mm (US 3) needles

TO FIT

One size

SKILL LEVEL

Intermediate

HAT

Using 3.00mm (US 2) needles and A,
cast on 120 sts. Divide sts evenly
across three dpns; join for working in
the round.

Round 1: With A, *k2, p2; rep from *
to end.

Round 2: As round 1.
Join in E.

Round 3: With E, *k2, p2; rep from *
to end.
Cut off E.

Rounds 4–9: As round 1.
Change to 3.25mm (US 3) needles.

Round 10: With A, *rib 1, inc in next st;
rep from * to end (180 sts).

Rounds 11–12: Knit.

Repeating the 12-st patt rep 15 times
around each round, work the 22 chart
rows twice.

Cut off all contrasts and cont using
A only.

Rounds 57–58: Knit.

SHAPE CROWN

Round 59: *K2, k2tog; rep from * to
end (135 sts).

Round 60: Knit.

Round 61: [K25, k2tog] 5 times
(130 sts).

Round 62: [K24, k2tog] 5 times
(125 sts).

Round 63: [K23, k2tog] 5 times
(120 sts).

Round 64: [K22, k2tog] 5 times
(115 sts).

Round 65: [K21, k2tog] 5 times
(110 sts).

Round 66: [K20, k2tog] 5 times
(105 sts).

Cont in this way, working one less st
between each decreases, until the foll
round has been worked:

Round 79: [K7, k2tog] 5 times
(40 sts).

Round 80: [K2tog] 20 times.
Break off yarn and thread through
rem 20 sts. Pull up tight and fasten
off securely.

FINISHING

Sew in all loose ends, block and press.
With one strand of each colour, make a
twisted cord approx. 14cm (5½ in) long
and knot one end to form a short tassel.
Attach other end of cord to top of Hat
as in photograph.

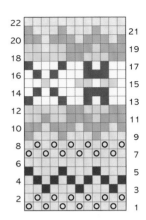

Key

	Oatmeal 025 (A) K on RS
⊙	Oatmeal 025 (A) P on RS
	Sea Green 006 (B) K on RS
	Porridge 024 (C) K on RS
	Peat 019 (D) K on RS
	Rust 009 (E) K on RS
	Gold 028 (F) K on RS

DESIGNED BY

Claire Garland

Rose cap

This cap may look a bit complicated for a beginner, but it's actually just combinations of plain knit and purl stitches and the basic increases and decreases. So if you are a new knitter, don't be afraid to give this pattern a go.

YARN

Debbie Bliss *Donegal Chunky Tweed* (100% pure new wool),
approx. 100g (3½oz)/100m (109yd) per skein

   1 skein of Peacock 09 (A)

Coats *Anchor Tapisserie Wool* (100% wool), approx. 10m
(11yd) per skein

   2 skeins of red 8202 (B)

   1 skein of burgundy 9274 (C)

NEEDLES

Pair of 4.50mm (US 7) knitting needles

Pair of 7.00mm (US 10½) knitting needles

TENSION (GAUGE)

12 sts and 18 rows = 10cm (4in) square measured over St st
using 7.00mm (US 10½) needles and A

TO FIT

One size

SKILL LEVEL

Beginner

HAT

Using 7.00mm (US 10½) needles and A, cast on 63 sts.

Row 1 (RS): K1, *p1, k1; rep from * to end.

Row 2: P1, *k1, p1; rep from * to end.

Rows 3–6: As rows 1–2, twice.

Row 7 (RS): [P20, inc in next st] 3 times (66 sts).

Row 8 and every foll alt row (to row 20): Knit.

Row 9: [Inc in next st, p10] 6 times (72 sts).

Row 11: [Inc in next st, p11] 6 times (78 sts).

Row 13: [Inc in next st, p12] 6 times (84 sts).

Row 15: [Inc in next st, p13] 6 times (90 sts).

Row 17: [Inc in next st, p14] 6 times (96 sts).

Row 19: [Inc in next st, p15] 6 times (102 sts).

Rows 20–21: Knit.

Row 22 and every foll alt row to end: Purl.

Row 23: K1, [k3tog, k7] 10 times, k1 (82 sts).

Row 25: Knit.

Row 27: K1, [k3tog, k5] 10 times, k1 (62 sts).

Row 29: Knit.

Row 31: K1, [k3tog, k3] 10 times, k1 (42 sts).

Row 33: Knit.

Row 35: K1, [k3tog, k1] 10 times, k1 (22 sts).

Row 37: Knit.

Row 39: [K2tog] 11 times.

Row 40: Purl.

Break off yarn and thread through rem 11 sts. Pull up tight and fasten off securely.

ROSE

Using 4.50mm (US 7) needles and B, cast on 80 sts.

Starting with a knit row, work in St st for 9 rows, ending with a WS row.

Cast (bind) off, leaving a long end.

LEAF

Using 4.50mm (US 7) needles and B, cast on 5 sts.

Row 1 (RS): K1, [inc in next st, k1] twice (7 sts).

Row 2: P7.

Row 3: K1, inc in next st, k3, inc in next st, k1 (9 sts).

Row 4: P9.

Row 5: K1, inc in next st, k5, inc in next st, k1 (11 sts).

Starting with a purl row, work in St st for 5 rows, ending with a WS row.

Row 11 (RS): K1, k2tog, k5, skpo, k1 (9 sts).

Row 12: P1, p2tog tbl, p3, p2tog, p1 (7 sts).

Row 13: K1, k2tog, k1, skpo, k1 (5 sts).

Row 14: P2tog tbl, p1, p2tog (3 sts).

Row 15: K3tog and fasten off.

FINISHING

Sew in all loose ends, block and press pieces, steaming Rose and Leaf quite hard to slightly felt them.

Sew back seam of Hat using mattress stitch. To form 'points', lay Hat flat and pinch each 'point' (where shaping occurs) and secure layers together with a few stitches on inside.

Roll up Rose strip to form a rose shape and, using the long end, secure cast (bound) off edges together at base of Rose. Sew Rose to Hat as in photograph, attaching Leaf next to it.

DESIGNED BY

Baker boy

A classic cap of the 1960s reinterpreted for the 21st century. The all-over texture pattern is easy to knit – just follow the pattern carefully for the first couple of rows and then it will be easy to see how the stitch repeat works.

YARN

Rowan Classic *Baby Alpaca DK* (100% baby alpaca), approx. 50g (1¾oz)/100m (109yd) per ball

 2 balls of Southdown 208

NEEDLES

Pair of 3.25mm (US 3) knitting needles

Pair of 3.75mm (US 5) knitting needles

EXTRAS

Piece of card 22cm (8½in) by 10cm (4in)

TENSION (GAUGE)

28 sts and 30 rows = 10cm (4in) square measured over patt using 3.75mm (US 5) needles

TO FIT

One size

SKILL LEVEL

Intermediate

CAP

Using 3.25mm (US 3) needles, cast on 108 sts.

Row 1 (RS): *K1, p1; rep from * to end.

Rows 2–9: As row 1.

Row 10 (WS): K1, m1, p1, *m1, k1, p1; rep from * to end (162 sts).

Change to 3.75mm (US 5) needles.

Now work in patt as follows:

Row 1 (RS): Purl.

Row 2: P1, *(k1, p1, k1) all into next st, p3tog; rep from * to last st, p1.

Row 3: Purl.

Row 4: P1, *p3tog, (k1, p1, k1) all into next st; rep from * to last st, p1.

Last 4 rows form patt.

Cont in patt for 26 rows more, ending after patt row 2 and with a WS row.

SHAPE CROWN

Row 1 (RS): P1, [sl 1, p4tog, psso, p15] 8 times, p1 (130 sts).

Work 3 rows.

Row 5: P1, [sl 1, p4tog, psso, p11] 8 times, p1 (98 sts).

Work 3 rows.

Row 9: P1, [sl 1, p4tog, psso, p7] 8 times, p1 (66 sts).

Work 3 rows.

Row 13: P1, [sl 1, p4tog, psso, p3] 8 times, p1 (34 sts).

Work 1 row.

Row 15: P1, [p2tog] 16 times, p1 (18 sts).

Row 16: P1, [p2tog] 8 times, p1. Break off yarn and thread through rem 10 sts. Pull up tight and fasten off securely.

LOWER PEAK

Using 3.25mm (US 3) needles, cast on 76 sts.

Row 1 (WS): Knit.

Rows 2–3: Knit to last 26 sts, turn.

Rows 4–5: Skpo, knit to last 24 sts, turn.

Rows 6–7: Skpo, knit to last 22 sts, turn.

Rows 8–9: Skpo, knit to last 20 sts, turn.

Rows 10–11: Skpo, knit to last 18 sts, turn.

Rows 12–13: Skpo, knit to last 16 sts, turn.

Rows 14–15: Skpo, knit to last 14 sts, turn.

Rows 16–17: Skpo, knit to last 12 sts, turn.

Rows 18–19: Skpo, knit to last 10 sts, turn.

Rows 20–21: Knit to last 8 sts, turn.

Rows 22–23: Knit to last 6 sts, turn.

Rows 24–25: Knit to last 4 sts, turn.

Rows 26–27: Knit to last 2 sts, turn.

Row 28: Knit.

Cast (bind) off.

UPPER PEAK

With RS facing and using 3.25mm (US 3) needles, pick up and knit 2 sts from first row-end edge of Lower Peak, 76 sts from cast on edge, then 2 sts from other row-end edge. 80 sts.

Row 1 (WS): Knit.

Rows 2–3: Knit to last 28 sts, turn.

Rows 4–5: Skpo, knit to last 26 sts, turn.

Complete as given for Lower Peak from row 4.

FINISHING

Sew in all loose ends. Do NOT press. Sew up back seam of Cap using mattress stitch.

Lay Peak flat and cut out this shape from card. Slip card inside Peak and join cast (bound) off edges, enclosing card. Sew joined Peak edges to cast on edge of rib section at front of Cap.

If you have never [...] shaping before, this is a g[...] project to learn it on. The cap p[...] uses a slightly simplified version of the technique and it is worked on straight needles rather than in the round, so you don't have the distraction of extra needles. When the pattern instructions say 'turn', simply swap the knitting needles in your hands so that you are ready to work back across the next row, even though you haven't reached the end of the first row. On the last row, knit across all the stitches.

Baker boy 65

TIP
worked short-row
reat.
eak.

DESIGNED BY

Beaded beanie

Fashionistas will adore this gothic beanie with its fluffy, beaded edging and over-size flower. Knit another flower the same and wear it as a corsage on your lapel or sew it to a ribbon and tie it around your wrist.

YARN

Rowan *Felted Tweed* (50% merino wool, 25% alpaca, 25% viscose), approx. 50g (1¾oz)/175m (191yd) per ball

   1 ball of Carbon 159 (A)

Rowan *Kidsilk Haze* (70% super kid mohair, 30% silk), approx. 25g (1oz)/210m (229yd) per ball

   1 ball of Wicked 599 (B)

NEEDLES

Pair of 3.00mm (US 3) knitting needles
Pair of 3.75mm (US 5) knitting needles

EXTRAS

Approx. 100 small black glass beads

TENSION (GAUGE)

23 sts and 32 rows = 10cm (4in) square measured over St st using 3.75mm (US 5) needles and A

TO FIT

One size

SKILL LEVEL

Intermediate

BEADING NOTE

Before starting, thread beads onto B. To do this, thread a fine sewing needle (one that will easily pass through the beads) with sewing thread. Knot ends of thread and then pass end of yarn through this loop. Thread a bead onto the sewing thread, then slide it along and onto the knitting yarn. Continue in this way until the required number of beads are on the yarn.

SPECIAL ABBREVIATIONS

See page 95 for information on B1.

HAT

Thread approx. 90 beads onto B.
Using 3.00mm (US 3) needles and
two strands of B held together, cast on
119 sts.

Row 1 (RS): K1, *p1, B1, p1, k1; rep
from * to last 2 sts, p1, k1.

Row 2: P1, *k1, p1; rep from * to end.

Row 3: K1, *p1, k1, p1, B1; rep from *
to last 2 sts, p1, k1.

Row 4: As row 2.

Row 5: As row 1.

Row 6: Inc in first st, k1, *p1, k1;
rep from * to last st, inc in last st
(121 sts).

Cut off B and join in A.

Change to 3.75mm (US 5) needles.

Starting with a knit row, work in St st
until Hat measures 10cm (4in), ending
with a WS row.

SHAPE CROWN

Row 1 (RS): [K10, k2tog] 10 times, k1
(111 sts).

Work 3 rows.

Row 5: [K9, k2tog] 10 times, k1
(101 sts).

Work 3 rows.

Row 9: [K8, k2tog] 10 times, k1
(91 sts).

Work 1 row.

Row 11: [K7, k2tog] 10 times, k1
(81 sts).

Work 1 row.

Row 13: [K6, k2tog] 10 times, k1
(71 sts).
Work 1 row.
Row 15: [K5, k2tog] 10 times, k1
(61 sts).
Work 1 row.
Row 17: [K4, k2tog] 10 times, k1
(51 sts).
Work 1 row.
Row 19: [K3, k2tog] 10 times, k1
(41 sts).
Work 1 row.
Row 21: [K2, k2tog] 10 times, k1
(31 sts).
Work 1 row.
Row 23: [K1, k2tog] 10 times, k1
(21 sts).
Work 1 row.
Row 25: [K2tog] 10 times, k1.
Break off yarn and thread through
rem 11 sts. Pull up tight and fasten
off securely.

FLOWER PETALS

Using 3.00mm (US 3) needles and
two strands of B held together, cast on
9 sts.
Row 1 (RS): K1, *p1, k1; rep from *
to end.
**Row 2: As row 1.
These 2 rows form moss (seed) st.
Keeping moss (seed) st correct, cont
as follows:

Row 3: K1, m1, moss (seed) st to end
(10 sts).
Work 1 row.
Rep last 2 rows once more (11 sts).
Work 2 rows without shaping.
Row 9: K2tog tbl, moss (seed) st to end
(10 sts).
Work 1 row.
Rep last 2 rows once more (9 sts).
Cast (bind) off 4 sts at beg of next row
(5 sts).
Work 1 row.****
Cast on 4 sts at beg of next row
(9 sts).***
Rep from ** to *** 4 times more, then
from ** to **** again.
Cast (bind) off rem 5 sts.

FLOWER CENTRE

Using 3.00mm (US 3) needles and A,
cast on 3 sts.
Row 1 (RS): K3.
Row 2 and every foll alt row: Purl.
Row 3: K1, [m1, k1] twice (5 sts).
Row 5: K1, m1, k3, m1, k1 (7 sts).
Row 7: K2tog, k3, k2tog (5 sts).
Row 9: K2tog, k1, k2tog (3 sts).
Row 10: P3.
Cast (bind) off.

FINISHING

Sew in all loose ends, block and press
the pieces, taking care not to damage
the beads.
Sew up back seam of Hat using
mattress stitch.
Join cast on and cast (bound) off ends
of Flower Petals. Run gathering threads
around straight row-end edge and pull
up to form flower. Sew Flower Centre in
place at centre of Flower Petals. Sew
completed flower to Hat as in
photograph, attaching rem beads to
Flower Centre.

TIP

Customise this hat design by
swapping the flower for a brooch
and choosing beads in a colour to
match it. Don't choose a very heavy
brooch or it will pull the knited
fabric out of shape.

DESIGNED BY

Sue Bradley

Bobble hat

A classic bobble hat is worked here in a chunky, quick-to-knit stitch pattern. The border is just simple stripes – it's the stitch texture that makes the striping look more intricate than it really is.

YARN

Rowan *Pure Wool Aran* (100% superwash wool), approx. 100g (3½oz)/170m (185yd) per ball

- 1 ball of Ivory 670 (A)
- 1 ball of Cedar 674 (B)
- 1 ball of Paper 671 (C)

NEEDLES

Pair of 5.00mm (US 8) knitting needles

TENSION (GAUGE)

24 sts and 28 rows = 10cm (4in) square measured over patt using 5.00mm (US 8) needles

TO FIT

One size

SKILL LEVEL

Beginner

HAT

With A, cast on 91 sts.

Row 1 (RS): *K2, p2; rep from * to last 3 sts, k2, p1.

Row 2: As row 1.

These 2 rows form patt.

Keeping patt correct and joining in and breaking off colours as required, now work in stripes as follows:

Rows 3–6: With A.

Row 7: With B.

Row 8: With C.

Rows 9–10: With A.

Row 11: With B.

Row 12: With C.

Rows 13–16: With A.

Rows 17–18: With B.

Rows 19–20: With C.

Cut off B and C and cont using A only.

Cont straight until Hat measures 18cm (7in), ending with a WS row.

SHAPE CROWN

Row 1 (RS): K1, *p2tog, p1, k1; rep from * to last 2 sts, p2tog (68 sts).

Rows 2–4: K1, *p2, k1; rep from * to last st, p1.

Row 5: K1, *p2tog, k1; rep from * to last st, p1 (46 sts).

Rows 6–8: *K1, p1; rep from * to end.

Row 9: K1, *k2tog; rep from * to last st, k1 (24 sts).

Row 10: *P2tog; rep from * to end (12 sts).

Row 11: *K2tog; rep from * to end (6 sts).

Break off yarn and thread through rem 6 sts. Pull up tight and fasten off securely.

FINISHING

Sew in all loose ends. Do NOT press. Sew back seam using mattress stitch, taking care to match up stripes.

With B, make a 9-cm (3½-in) diameter pom-pom and attach to top of hat as in photograph.

DESIGNED BY

Carol Meldrum

Paris beret

As chic as the city it's named for, you can wear this beret with denims, with a fitted dress, with a slim-line coat – anything with a sleek silhouette. The herringbone pattern border defines the shaping and adds understated texture.

YARN
Rowan *Kid Classic* (70% lambswool, 26% kid mohair, 4% nylon), approx. 50g (1¾oz)/140m (153yd) per ball
   1 ball of Feather 828

NEEDLES
Pair of 3.75mm (US 5) knitting needles
Pair of 5.00mm (US 8) knitting needles

TENSION (GAUGE)
18 sts and 25 rows = 10cm (4in) square measured over St st using 5.00mm (US 8) needles

TO FIT
One size

SKILL LEVEL
Intermediate

HAT

Using 3.75mm (US 5) needles, cast on
111 sts.

Row 1 (RS): K1, *p1, k1; rep from *
to end.

Row 2: P1, *k1, p1; rep from * to end.
These 2 rows form rib.

Cont in rib for 10 rows more, dec 1 st
at end of last row and ending with a
WS row (110 sts).

Change to 5.00mm (US 8) needles.
Now work in herringbone patt
as follows:

Row 13 (RS): K1, *sl 1, k1, psso but
leave this st on LH needle point, now
knit into back of this (slipped) st; rep
from * to end.

Row 14: *P2tog leaving sts on LH
needle, then purl first of these 2 sts
again and slip both sts off LH needle;
rep from * to end.

These 2 rows form herringbone patt.
Work in the herringbone patt for
6 rows more.

Row 21 (RS): K1, m1, knit to end
(111 sts).

Row 22: Purl.

Row 23: [K10, m1] 11 times, k1
(122 sts).

Row 24: Purl.

Row 25: Knit.

Row 26: Purl.

Row 27: [K11, m1] 11 times, k1
(133 sts).

Rows 28–30: As rows 24–26, inc 1 st
at end of last row (134 sts).

Rows 31–32: As rows 13–14.

SHAPE CROWN

Row 33: K1, [k10, skpo] 11 times, k1
(123 sts).

Row 34 and every foll alt row: Purl.

Row 35: Knit.

Row 37: K1, [k9, skpo] 11 times, k1
(112 sts).

Row 39: Knit.

Row 41: K1, [k8, skpo] 11 times, k1
(101 sts).

Row 43: Knit.

Row 45: K1, [k7, skpo] 11 times, k1
(90 sts).

Row 47: K1, [k6, skpo] 11 times, k1
(79 sts).

Row 49: K1, [k5, skpo] 11 times, k1
(68 sts).

Row 51: K1, [k4, skpo] 11 times, k1
(57 sts).

Row 53: K1, [k3, skpo] 11 times, k1
(46 sts).

Row 55: K1, [k2, skpo] 11 times, k1
(35 sts).

Row 57: K1, [k1, skpo] 11 times, k1
(24 sts).

Row 58: Purl.

Break off yarn and thread through
rem 24 sts. Pull up tight and fasten
off securely.

FINISHING

Sew in all loose ends, block and press.
Sew back seam using mattress stitch.

DESIGNED BY

Beaded beret

Beading brings instant glamour to knitting, as you can see from this fabulous beret.
This isn't a remotely difficult technique to master – if you can knit then you can bead
knit – so choose your beads and get going.

YARN

Rowan *4-ply Soft* (100% merino wool), approx. 50g
(1¾oz)/175m (191yd) per ball

  2 balls of Tea Rose 401

NEEDLES

Set of four 3.25mm (US 3) double-pointed needles

EXTRAS

Approx. 750 Rowan clear glass beads, ref J3001008

Six stitch markers

Length of 7mm (¼in) wide elastic to fit around head

TENSION (GAUGE)

28 sts and 36 rows = 10cm (4in) square measured over St st
using 3.25mm (US 3) needles

TO FIT

One size

SKILL LEVEL

Intermediate

SPECIAL ABBREVIATIONS

See page 95 for information on B1.

BEADING NOTE

Before starting, thread beads onto yarn. To do this, thread a fine sewing needle (one that will easily pass through the beads) with sewing thread. Knot ends of thread and then pass end of yarn through this loop. Thread a bead onto the sewing thread, then gently slide it along and onto the knitting yarn. Continue in this way until the required number of beads are on the yarn.

MAIN SECTION

Cast on 156 sts. Divide sts evenly across three dpns; join for working in the round.

Round 1: [K26, PM] 6 times.

Round 2: *K1, B1, m1, [k3, m1] 7 times, B1, k1, B1, SM to RH needle; rep from * 5 times more (204 sts).

Round 3: [K12, B1, k1, B1, k3, B1, k1, B1, k13, SM to RH needle] 6 times.

Round 4: [K11, B1, k3, B1, k1, B1, k3, B1, k11, B1, SM to RH needle] 6 times.

Round 5: [K16, B1, k17, SM to RH needle] 6 times.

Round 6: [K11, B1, k9, B1, k12, SM to RH needle] 6 times.

Round 7: [K7, m1, k5, B1, k7, B1, k5, m1, k8, SM to RH needle] 6 times (216 sts).

Round 8: [K8, B1, k1, B1, k3, B1, k5,
B1, k3, B1, k1, B1, k9, SM to RH needle] 6 times.

Round 9: *K7, [B1, k3] 5 times, B1, k8, SM to RH needle; rep from * 5 times more.

Round 10: [K12, B1, k3, B1, k1, B1, k3, B1, k13, SM to RH needle] 6 times.

Round 11: *K7, B1, k5, [B1, k3] twice, B1, k5, B1, k8, SM to RH needle; rep from * 5 times more.

Round 12: *K7, m1, k1, [B1, k5] 3 times, B1, k1, m1, k8, SM to RH needle; rep from * 5 times more (228 sts).

Round 13: [K10, B1, k5, B1, k3, B1, k5, B1, k11, SM to RH needle] 6 times.

Round 14: *K9, [B1, k5] 3 times, B1, k10, SM to RH needle; rep from * 5 times more.

Round 15: [K8, B1, k5, B1, k3, B1, k3, B1, k5, B1, k9, SM to RH needle] 6 times.

Round 16: [K13, B1, k3, B1, k1, B1, k3, B1, k14, SM to RH needle] 6 times.

Round 17: *K7, m1, k1, [B1, k3] 5 times, B1, k1, m1, k8, SM to RH needle; rep from * 5 times more (240 sts).

Round 18: [K10, B1, k1, B1, k3, B1, k5, B1, k3, B1, k1, B1, k11, SM to RH needle] 6 times.

Round 19: [K15, B1, k7, B1, k16, SM to RH needle] 6 times.

Round 20: [K14, B1, k9, B1, k15, SM to RH needle] 6 times.

Round 21: [K19, B1, k20, SM to RH needle] 6 times.

Round 22: [K7, m1, k7, B1, k3, B1, k1, B1, k3, B1, k7, m1, k8, SM to RH needle] 6 times (252 sts).

Round 23: [K16, B1, k1, B1, k3, B1, k1, B1, k17, SM to RH needle] 6 times.

Round 24: [K36, wrap next st (by slipping next st from LH needle to RH needle, taking yarn to opposite side of work between needles and then slipping same st back onto LH needle – when working back across wrapped sts, work the wrapped st and the wrapping loop tog as one st) and turn, p31, wrap next st and turn, k21, wrap next st and turn, p11, wrap next st and turn, k16, wrap next st and turn, p21, wrap next st and turn, k29, wrap next st and turn, p37, wrap next st and turn, k40, SM to RH needle] 6 times.

Round 25: Knit.

Round 26: [skpo, k37, k2tog, k1, SM to RH needle] 6 times (240 sts).

Rounds 27–28: Knit.

Round 29: [Skpo, k17, B1, k17, k2tog, k1, SM to RH needle] 6 times (228 sts).

Round 30: Knit.

Round 31: [K18, B1, k19] 6 times.

Round 32: [Skpo, k33, k2tog, k1, SM to RH needle] 6 times (216 sts).

Round 33: [K17, B1, k18] 6 times.

Round 34: Knit.

Round 35: *Skpo, k13, [B1, k1] twice, B1, k13, k2tog, k1, SM to RH needle; rep from * 5 times more (204 sts).

Round 36: Knit.

Round 37: *K12, [B1, k3] twice, B1, k13, SM to RH needle; rep from * 5 times more.

Round 38: [Skpo, k29, k2tog, k1, SM to RH needle] 6 times (192 sts).

Round 39: *K9, [B1, k5] twice, B1, k10, SM to RH needle; rep from * 5 times more.

Round 40: Knit.

Round 41: *Skpo, k5, [B1, k7] twice, B1, k5, k2tog, k1, SM to RH needle; rep from * 5 times more (180 sts).

Round 42: Knit.

Round 43: *K12, [B1, k1] twice, B1, k13, SM to RH needle; rep from * 5 times more.

Round 44: [Skpo, k25, k2tog, k1, SM to RH needle] 6 times (168 sts).

Round 45: *K9, [B1, k3] twice, B1, k10, SM to RH needle; rep from * 5 times more.

Round 46: Knit.

Round 47: *Skpo, k5, [B1, k5] 3 times, k2tog, k1, SM to RH needle; rep from *

5 times more (156 sts).

Round 48: Knit.

Round 49: [K12, B1, k13, SM to RH needle] 6 times.

Round 50: [Skpo, k21, k2tog, k1, SM to RH needle] 6 times (144 sts).

Round 51: *K9, [B1, k1] twice, B1, k10, SM to RH needle; rep from * 5 times more.

Round 52: Knit.

Round 53: *Skpo, k5, [B1, k3] twice, B1, k5, k2tog, k1, SM to RH needle; rep from * 5 times more (132 sts).

Round 54: Knit.

Round 55: [K10, B1, k11, SM to RH needle] 6 times.

Round 56: [Skpo, k17, k2tog, k1, SM to RH needle] 6 times (120 sts).

Round 57: [K9, B1, k10, SM to RH needle] 6 times.

Round 58: Knit.

Round 59: *Skpo, k5, [B1, k1] twice, B1, k5, k2tog, k1, SM to RH needle; rep from * 5 times more (108 sts).

Round 60: Knit.

Round 61: [K8, B1, k9, SM to RH needle] 6 times.

Round 62: [Skpo, k13, k2tog, k1, SM to RH needle] 6 times (96 sts).

Round 63: [K7, B1, k8, SM to RH needle] 6 times.

Round 64: [Skpo, k11, k2tog, k1, SM to RH needle] 6 times (84 sts).

Round 65: [K6, B1, k7, SM to RH needle] 6 times.

Round 66: [Skpo, k9, k2tog, k1, SM to RH needle] 6 times (72 sts).

Round 67: Knit.

Round 68: [Skpo, k7, k2tog, k1, SM to RH needle] 6 times (60 sts).

Round 69: Knit.

Round 70: [Skpo, k5, k2tog, k1, SM to RH needle] 6 times (48 sts).

Round 71: Knit.

Round 72: [Skpo, k3, k2tog, k1, SM to RH needle] 6 times (36 sts).

Round 73: Knit.

Round 74: [Skpo, k1, k2tog, k1, SM to RH needle] 6 times (24 sts).

Round 75: Knit.

Round 76: [sl 1, k2tog, psso, k1, remove M] 6 times.

Break off yarn and thread through rem 12 sts. Pull up tight and fasten off securely.

BAND

With RS facing, pick up and knit 156 sts around cast on edge of Main Section. Divide sts evenly across three dpns and work in rounds as follows:

Round 1: Knit.

Rep this round until Band measures 4cm (1½in) from pick-up round.

Cast (bind) off.

FINISHING

Sew in all loose ends, block and press fabric, taking great care not to damage beads.

Join ends of elastic to form a ring. Fold Band in half to inside and neatly sew cast (bound) off edge to pick-up round, enclosing elastic in this casing.

Make a 7cm (2¾in) long tassel and separate strands of yarn within tassel. Attach tassel to centre of crown.

TIP

If you want to use different beads to those stated in the pattern that's fine, but there are a couple of simple rules to follow. Firstly, the hole in the beads must be large enough to slip over doubled yarn so that you can thread the beads onto the yarn. If doesn't matter if they are a tight fit on doubled yarn as they only need to travel over a short distance of this before they slide onto the single thickness of yarn. Secondly, the beads must not be larger than the knitted stitch or they won't lie neat and flat against the knitted fabric. Knit a tension (gauge) swatch and take it with you to the bead shop with you when buying your beads. Lay one of your chosen beads on the swatch and check it fits within a stitch before buying.

DESIGNED BY

Cluster hat

Vivid colours and chunky crochet clusters combine to make this cute pull-on hat. It is crocheted in rounds as a simple stripy tube and when the top edge is joined with crochet, the kitty-cat ears appear.

YARN

Coats *Anchor Tapisserie Wool* (100% wool), approx. 10m
(11yd) per skein

 3 skeins of cornflower 8630 (A)

 2 skeins of nut 9448 (B)

 2 skeins of pine 8992 (C)

 3 skeins of tangerine 8192 (D)

 2 skeins of pale turquoise 8192 (E)

 2 skeins of violet 8932 (F)

 2 skeins of buttercup 8156 (**G**)

 2 skeins of custard 8018 (**H**)

 3 skeins of ginger 9558 (**I**)

 2 skeins of cyclamen 8486 (**J**)

 2 skeins of red rose 8440 (**K**)

 2 skeins of leaf green 9098 (**L**)

 2 skeins of deep lilac 8594 (**M**)

 2 skeins of pale pink 8482 (**N**)

NEEDLES

4.50mm (G/6) crochet hook

EXTRAS

One button

TENSION (GAUGE)

7 clusters and 7 rows = 10cm (4in) square measured over
patt using 4.50mm (G/6) hook

TO FIT

One size

SKILL LEVEL

Intermediate

SPECIAL ABBREVIATIONS

See page 95 for information on cluster, tr3tog (dc3tog).

HAT

With A, make 88 ch and join with a ss (sl st) to form a ring.

Round 1: 1 ch (does NOT count as st), 1 dc (sc) into each ch to end, ss (sl st) to first dc (sc), turn (88 sts).

Rounds 2–4: 1 ch (does NOT count as st), 1 dc (sc) into each dc (sc) to end, ss (sl st) to first dc (sc), turn.

Change to B.

Round 5: With B, 3 ch (does NOT count as st), 1 tr (dc) into dc (sc) at base of 3 ch, *1 ch, miss 1 dc (sc), 1 cluster into next dc (sc); rep from * to last dc (sc), 1 ch, miss last dc (sc), ss (sl st) to top of tr (dc) at beg of round. Joining in and breaking off colours as required, now work in patt as follows:

Round 6: With C, ss (sl st) into first ch sp, 3 ch (does NOT count as st), 1 tr (dc) into same ch sp, *1 ch, miss 1 cluster, 1 cluster into next ch sp; rep from * to last cluster, 1 ch, miss last cluster, ss (sl st) to top of tr (dc) at beg of round.

This round forms patt.

Keeping patt correct, now work in stripes as follows:

Rounds 7–8: With D.
Round 9: With E.
Round 10: With F.
Round 11: With G.
Round 12: With H.
Round 13: With A.
Rounds 14–15: With I.
Round 16: With J.
Round 17: With K.
Round 18: With L.
Round 19: With M.
Round 20: With N.

Change to D.

Fold Hat flat and join top seam by working a row of dc (sc) with D across top of last round, working each dc (sc) through both layers and working 1 dc (sc) into each ch sp and cluster. Fasten off.

FLOWER

With F, make 33 ch.

Row 1: 1 tr (dc) into 3rd ch from hook, 1 tr (dc) into each ch to end.

Fasten off, leaving a fairly long end. Roll strip up to form a flower shape and secure along foundation ch edge to form base of Flower.

LEAF

With L, make 14 ch.

Row 1: 2 tr (dc) into 4th ch from hook, 1 tr (dc) into each of next 2 ch, tr3tog (dc3tog) over next 3 ch, turn.

Row 2: 1 dc (sc) into top of tr3tog (dc3tog), 1 dc (sc) into each of next 4 tr (dc), 1 dc (sc) into next ch, now working back along foundation ch edge: 1 tr (dc) into each of next 5 ch, tr3tog (dc3tog) over next 3 ch, turn, miss tr3tog (dc3tog), 1 ss (sl st) into next tr (dc). Fasten off.

FINISHING

Sew in all loose ends, block and press. Using photograph as a guide, roll back brim and secure in place. Pinch upper corners of Hat and secure with a few small stitches to form cat ears as in photograph. Attach Flower to rolled-back brim section, positioning button at centre. Attach Leaf next to Flower.

Knitting

TENSION (GAUGE) AND SELECTING CORRECT NEEDLE SIZE

Tension (gauge) can differ quite dramatically between knitters. This is because of the way that the needles and the yarn are held. So if your tension (gauge) does not match that stated in the pattern, you should change your needle size following this simple rule:

- If your knitting is too loose, your tension (gauge) will read that you have fewer stitches and rows than the given tension (gauge), and you will need to change to a smaller needle to make the stitch size smaller.
- If your knitting is too tight, your tension (gauge) will read that you have more stitches and rows than the given tension (gauge), and you will need to change to a thicker needle to make the stitch size bigger.

Please note that if the projects in this book are not knitted to the correct tension (gauge), yarn quantities will be affected.

KNITTING A TENSION (GAUGE) SWATCH

No matter how excited you are about a new knitting project, take time to knit a tension (gauge) swatch for accurate sizing. Use the same needles, yarn and stitch pattern as those that will be used for the main work and knit a sample at least 12.5cm (5in) square. Smooth out the finished piece on a flat surface, but do not stretch it.

To check the stitch tension (gauge), place a ruler horizontally on the sample, measure 10cm (4in) across and mark with a pin at each end. Count the number of stitches between the pins. To check the row tension (gauge), place a ruler vertically on the sample, measure 10cm (4in) and mark with pins. Count the number of rows between the pins. If the number of stitches and rows is greater than specified in the pattern, make a new swatch using larger needles; if it is less, make a new swatch using smaller needles.

MAKING A SLIP KNOT

A slip knot is the basis of all casting-on techniques and is therefore the starting point for almost everything you do in knitting and crochet.

1

1 Wind the yarn around two fingers twice as shown. Insert a knitting needle through the first (front) strand and under the second (back) one.

2

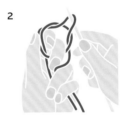

2 Using the needle, pull the back strand through the front one to form a loop.

3

3 Holding the loose ends of the yarn with your left hand, pull the needle upwards, thus tightening the knot. Pull the ball end of the yarn again to tighten the knot further.

CASTING ON

'Casting on' is the term used for making a row of stitches to be used as a foundation for your knitting.

1

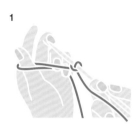

1 Make a slip knot 100cm (40in) from the end of the yarn. Hold the needle in your right hand with the ball end of the yarn over your index finger. *Wind the loose end of the yarn around your left thumb from front to back.

2

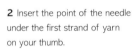

2 Insert the point of the needle under the first strand of yarn on your thumb.

3 With your right index finger, take the ball end of the yarn over the point of the needle.

3

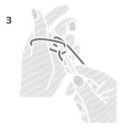

4 Pull a loop through to form the first stitch. Remove your left thumb from the yarn. Pull the loose end to secure the stitch. Repeat from * until the required number of stitches have been cast on.

4

THE BASIC STITCHES

Knit and purl stitches form the basis of all knitted fabrics. The knit stitch is the easiest to learn and once you have mastered this you can move on to the purl stitch, which is the reverse of the knit stitch.

KNIT STITCH

1

1 Hold the needle with the cast-on stitches in your left hand, with the loose yarn at the back of the work. Insert the right-hand needle from left to right through the front of the first stitch on the left-hand needle.

2

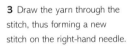

2 Wrap the yarn from left to right over the point of the right-hand needle.

3 Draw the yarn through the stitch, thus forming a new stitch on the right-hand needle.

3

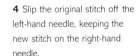

4 Slip the original stitch off the left-hand needle, keeping the new stitch on the right-hand needle.

5 To knit a row, repeat steps 1 to 4 until all the stitches have been transferred from the left-hand needle to the right-hand needle. Turn the work, transferring the needle with the stitches to your left hand to work the next row.

4

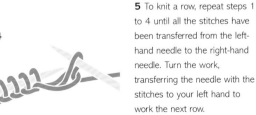

PURL STITCH

1

2

3

4

1 Hold the needle with the stitches in your left hand, with the loose yarn at the front of the work. Insert the right-hand needle from right to left into the front of the first stitch on the left-hand needle.

2 Wrap the yarn from right to left, up and over the point of the right-hand needle.

3 Draw the yarn through the stitch, thus forming a new stitch on the right-hand needle.

4 Slip the original stitch off the left-hand needle, keeping the new stitch on the right-hand needle.

5 To purl a row, repeat steps 1 to 4 until all the stitches have been transferred from the left-hand needle to the right-hand needle. Turn the work, transferring the needle with the stitches to your left hand to work the next row.

- -

INCREASING AND DECREASING

Many projects will require some shaping, either just to add interest or to make the various sections fit together properly. Shaping is achieved by increasing or decreasing the number of stitches you are working.

INCREASING

The simplest method of increasing one stitch is to work into the front and back of the same stitch.

On a knit row, knit into the front of the stitch to be increased, then before slipping it off the needle, place the right-hand needle behind the left-hand one and knit again into the back of it (inc). Slip the original stitch off the left-hand needle. On a purl row, purl into the front of the stitch to be increased, then before slipping it off the needle, purl again into the back of it. Slip the original stitch off the left-hand needle.

DECREASING

The simplest method of decreasing one stitch is to work two stitches together.

On a knit row, insert the right-hand needle from left to right through two stitches instead of one, then knit them together as one stitch. This is called knit two together (k2tog).

On a purl row, insert the right-hand needle from right to left through two stitches instead of one, then purl them together as one stitch. This is called purl two together (p2tog).

INTARSIA STITCHES

'Intarsia' is where the pattern is worked in large blocks of colour at a time, requiring a separate ball of yarn for each area of colour.

DIAGONAL COLOUR CHANGE WITH A SLANT TO THE LEFT

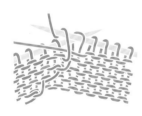

On a wrong-side row, with the yarns at the front of the work, take the first colour over the second colour, drop it, then pick up the second colour underneath the first colour, thus crossing the two colours over one another.

DIAGONAL COLOUR CHANGE WITH A SLANT TO THE RIGHT

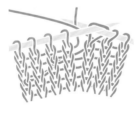

On a right-side row, with the yarns at the back of the work, take the first colour over the second colour, drop it, then pick up the second colour underneath the first colour, thus crossing the two colours.

VERTICAL COLOUR CHANGE

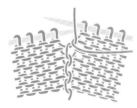

Work in the first colour to the colour change, then drop the first colour, pick up the second colour underneath the first colour, crossing the two colours over before working the next stitch in the second colour. After a colour change, work the first stitch firmly to prevent a gap forming between colours.

FAIR ISLE STITCHES

Yarn that is not in use is left at the back of the work until needed. The loops formed by this are called 'floats' and it is important that they are not pulled too tightly when working the next stitch, as this will pull your knitting.

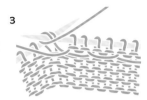

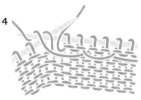

1 On a knit row, hold the first colour in your right hand and the second colour in your left hand. Knit the required number of stitches as usual with the first colour, carrying the second colour loosely across the wrong side of the work.

2 To knit a stitch in the second colour, insert the right-hand needle into the next stitch, then draw a loop through from the yarn held in the left hand, carrying the yarn in the right hand loosely across the wrong side until required.

3 On a purl row, hold the yarns as for the knit rows. Purl the required number of stitches as usual with the first colour, carrying the second colour loosely across these stitches on the wrong side of the work.

4 To purl a stitch in the second colour, insert the right-hand needle into the next stitch, then draw a loop through from the yarn held in the left hand, carrying the yarn in the right hand loosely across the wrong side until next required.

CASTING (BINDING) OFF

This is the most commonly used method of securing stitches at the end of a piece of knitting. The cast-off edge should have the same 'give' or elasticity as the fabric; cast (bind) off in the stitch used for the main fabric unless the pattern directs otherwise.

KNITWISE

Knit two stitches. *Using the point of the left-hand needle, lift the first stitch on the right-hand needle over the second, then drop it off the needle. Knit the next stitch and repeat from * until all stitches have been worked off the left-hand needle and only one stitch remains on the right-hand needle. Cut the yarn, leaving enough to sew in the end. Thread the end through the stitch, then slip it off the needle. Draw the yarn up firmly to fasten off.

PURLWISE

Purl two stitches. *Using the point of the left-hand needle, lift the first stitch on the right-hand needle over the second and drop it off the needle. Purl the next stitch and repeat from * until all the stitches have been worked off the left-hand needle and only one stitch remains on the right-hand needle. Cut the yarn, leaving enough to sew in the end. Thread the end through the stitch, then slip it off the needle. Draw the yarn up firmly to fasten off.

Crochet

TENSION (GAUGE)

This is the number of rows and stitches per centimetre or inch, usually measured over a 10cm (4in) square. The tension (gauge) will determine the size of the finished item. The correct tension (gauge) is given at the beginning of each pattern. Crochet a small swatch, using the recommended yarn and hook, to make sure you are working to the correct tension (gauge). If your work is too loose, choose a hook that is one size smaller, and if it is too tight, choose a hook the next size up. When making clothes, it is important to check tension (gauge) before you start; it is not worth making something the wrong size. When measuring work, lay it on a flat surface and always measure at the centre, rather than at the side edges.

- -

BASIC STITCHES

Start by making a series of chains – around 10 will be enough. Now you're ready to practise the following stitches.

SLIP STITCH (SS) (SL ST)

1 This is the shortest stitch and mostly used for joining and shaping. Insert the hook into a stitch or chain (always remember to insert the hook under both strands of the stitch), yarn over the hook from the back to the front of the hook, and draw the hook through the stitch and the loop on the hook. You are left with just 1 loop on the hook. This is 1 slip stitch.

DOUBLE CROCHET (DC) (SINGLE CROCHET (SC))

1 Insert the hook into the second chain from the hook, yarn over the hook, draw the loop through your work.

2 Yarn over and draw the hook through both loops on the hook; 1 loop on the hook. This is 1 double crochet.

3 Repeat into the next stitch or chain until you've reached the end of the row, make 1 chain stitch – this is your turning chain – turn the work and work 1 double crochet (single crochet) into each stitch of the previous row, ensuring that you insert the hook under both loops of the stitch you are crocheting into.

HALF TREBLE CROCHET (HTR) (HALF DOUBLE CROCHET (HDC))

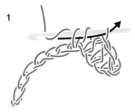

1 Yarn over the hook before inserting the hook into the third chain from the hook, yarn over, draw 1 loop through the work, yarn over, draw through all 3 loops on the hook; 1 loop on the hook. This is 1 half treble crochet (half double crochet).

2 When you reach the end of the row, make 2 chains – this counts as the first stitch of the next row. Turn the work, skip the first half treble crochet (half double crochet) of the previous row and insert the hook into the second stitch of the new row. Continue to work until the end of the row. At the end of the row, work the last half treble (half double) into the top of the turning chain of the row below.

TREBLE CROCHET (TR)
(DOUBLE CROCHET (DC))

1 Start by wrapping the yarn over the hook and insert the hook into the fourth chain from the hook, yarn over, draw 1 loop through the work

2 Yarn over, draw through the first 2 loops on the hook, yarn over, draw through the remaining 2 loops on the hook; 1 loop on the hook. This is 1 treble crochet (double crochet).

3 When you reach the end of the row, make 3 chains. These count as the first stitch of the next row. Turn the work and skip the first treble crochet (double crochet) of the previous row; insert the hook into the second stitch of the new row. Continue to work until the end of the row, inserting the last treble crochet (double crochet) into the top of the turning chain of the row below.

1

2

BASIC TECHNIQUES

As well as working from right to left in rows, crochet can also be worked in a circular fashion (referred to as working in the round), or even in a continuous spiral to make seamless items such as hats, bags and other rounded objects.

MAKING FABRIC – WORKING IN ROWS

1

2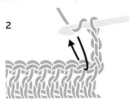

3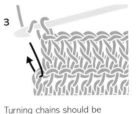

1 Make as many chain stitches as you require. This row is called the base chain. Insert the hook into the second chain from the hook (not counting the chain on the hook) for double crochet (single crochet), third chain from the hook for treble crochet (double crochet)

2 Work from right to left, inserting the hook under two of the three threads in each chain.

3 When you reach the end of the row, work one or more turning chains, depending on the height of the stitch.

Turning chains should be worked as follows:
Double (single) crochet: 1 chain.
Half treble (half double): 2 chains.
Treble (double): 3 chains.
Double treble (treble): 4 chains.
Triple treble (double treble): 5 chains.

Now turn the work to begin working on the next row (remember always to turn your work in the same direction). When working in double crochet (single crochet), insert the hook into the first stitch in the new row and work each stitch to the end of the row, excluding the turning chain. For all other stitches, unless the pattern states otherwise, the turning chain counts as the first stitch. Skip 1 stitch and work each stitch to the end of the row, including the top of the turning chain.

MAKING FABRIC – WORKING IN THE ROUND

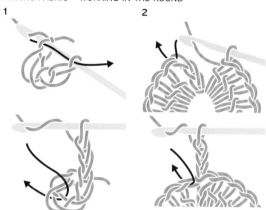

1 Crochet in the round starts with a ring. To make a ring, make a series of chains and join the last chain to the first with a slip stitch.

2 To make the first round, work a starting chain to the height of the stitch you are working in. Then work as many stitches as you need into the centre of the ring and finish the round with a slip stitch into the first stitch.

3 Begin the second and subsequent rounds with a starting chain (worked the same way as a turning chain, with the number of chains depending on the stitch you are working: see page 92). Then insert the hook under the top 2 loops of each stitch in the previous round. At the end of the round, join to the top of the starting chain with a slip stitch, as in step 2.

INCREASING

As with knitting, fabric is often shaped by increasing the number of stitches in a row or round. To increase, simply work an additional stitch into the next stitch. A single increase is made by working 2 stitches into the same stitch. You can of course increase by more than 1 stitch at a time.

DECREASING

DC2TOG (SC2TOG)

To decrease 1 stitch in double crochet (dc2tog) (single crochet (sc2tog)), insert hook into next stitch, yarn over, draw through the work, insert hook into the next stitch, yarn over, draw through the work, yarn over, draw through all 3 loops, leaving just 1 loop on the hook.

DC3TOG (SC3TOG)

To decrease by 2 stitches in double crochet (single crochet), work 3 stitches together, dc3tog (sc3tog), by working as for dc2tog (sc2tog) until you have 3 loops on the hook. Insert the hook into the next stitch, yarn over, draw through the work, yarn over and draw through all 4 loops.

TR2TOG (DC2TOG)

To decrease 1 stitch in treble crochet (tr2tog) (double crochet (dc2tog)), yarn over, insert hook into next stitch, yarn over, draw through work, yarn over, draw through 2 loops, yarn over, insert hook into next stitch, yarn over, draw through work, yarn over, draw through 2 loops, yarn over, draw through all 3 loops.

FINISHING OFF

Once you have fastened off, this is a useful way of sewing up crochet seams.

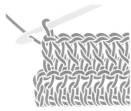

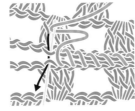

FASTENING OFF

Cut the yarn, leaving roughly 13cm (5in). Make 1 chain and draw the tail through the chain and pull firmly. Weave the end a few centimetres or an inch in one direction and then back the other way for a neat and secure finish.

FLAT STITCH

This seam creates an almost invisible join. Lay the two sections right-side up, with the stitches aligned. Using a tapestry needle, insert under the lower half of the edge stitch on one section, then under the upper half of the edge stitch on the opposite section.

Abbreviations

KNITTING ABBREVIATIONS

alt = alternate/alternating
beg = beginning
cn = cable needle
cont = continue
dec = decrease/decreasing
dpn = double-pointed needle
foll = following
inc = increase/increasing
k = knit
k2tog = knit two together
LH = left-hand
M = marker
m1 = make one st. Lift the horizontal strand between the st just worked and next st, then knit through back of this thread.
p = purl
p2tog = purl two together
patt = pattern
PM = place marker
prev = previous
psso = pass slipped stitch over
rem = remain/remaining
rep = repeat
Rev st st = reverse stocking (stockinette) stitch
RH = right-hand
RS = right side
skpo = slip 1 st knitwise, knit 1 st, pass slipped stitch over

sl = slip
SM = slip marker
St st = stocking (stockinette) stitch
st(s) = stitch(es)
tbl = through back of loops
tog = together
TS = thumb section
WS = wrong side
yfwd = yarn forward
yon = yarn over needle
yrn = yarn round needle

CROCHET ABBREVIATIONS

ch = chain
cluster = [yoh and insert hook as indicated, yoh and draw loops through, yoh and draw through first loop, yoh and draw through 2 loops] twice, yoh and draw through all 3 loops on hook
dc = double crochet
dtr = double treble
htr = half treble
sc = single crochet
sp(s) = space(s)
ss = slip stitch
tr = treble
tr tr = triple treble

tr3tog = [yoh and insert hook as indicated, yoh and draw loop through, yoh and draw through 2 loops] 3 times, yoh and draw through all 4 loops on hook

tr5tog = [yoh and insert hook as indicated, yoh and draw loop through, yoh and draw through 2 loops] 5 times, yoh and draw through all 6 loops on hook

qtr = quintuple treble. [yoh] 5 times, insert hook as indicated, yoh and draw loop through, [yoh and draw through 2 loops] 6 times

yoh = yarn over hook

SPECIAL ABBREVIATIONS

BE SEEN BERET

MK = insert RH needle under strand running between first and second sts on LH needle and loosely draw loop through, insert RH needle above same strand between sts and loosely draw through a second loop, bring yarn to front (RS) of work, p1, lift the 2 loops over this p st and off RH needle

CLUSTER HAT

cluster = [yoh and insert hook as indicated, yoh and draw loops through, yoh and draw through first loop, yoh and draw through 2 loops] twice, yoh and draw through all 3 loops on hook

tr3tog = [yoh and insert hook as indicated, yoh and draw loop through, yoh and draw through 2 loops] 3 times, yoh and draw through all 4 loops on hook

BEADED BERET

B1 = bring yarn to front (RS) of work, slip a bead up close to stitch just worked, slip next stitch purlwise then take yarn back to back (WS) of work, leaving bead sitting in front of slipped stitch

SEWING SEAMS

If you are sewing up a straight seam, then mattress stitch works well.

Lay the pieces right side up and next to each other. You are going to work up the side of the knitted pieces between the edge stitch and the next stitch, the edge stitch from each side will dissapear into the seam. Put the tapestry needle in between the edge and next stitch on one knitted piece and take it up the coloumn between the edge stitch and next stitch, going under two stitch bars.. Move over to the other piece and do the same. Go back to the point where the needle came out on the first piece and put it back in, going up the column under the next two bars. Continue going back and forth and pulling the thread tight each time. You will see that the two edges are pulled together.

SEWING IN ENDS

Once your hat has been sewn together the yarn ends need to be sewn into the seams. One at a time, thread the yarn ends into a tapestry needle and weave them into the seam. Cut off the end of the yarn.

Resources

Alchemy
PO Box 1080
Sebastopol
CA 95473
USA
+1 707 823 3276
www.alchemyyarns.com

Coats
PO Box 22
Lingfield House
Lingfield Point
McMullen Road
Darlington
County Durham DL1 1YQ
England, United Kingdom
01325 394237
www.coatscrafts.co.uk

Debbie Bliss Yarns
c/o Designer Yarns Ltd.
Unit 8-10 Newbridge
Industrial Estate
Pitt Street
Keighley
West Yorkshire
BD21 4PQ
01535 664222
www.designeryarns.uk.com

GGH
Mühlenstraße 74
25421 Pinneberg
Germany
+49 (0)4101 208484
www.ggh-garn.de

Jamieson & Smith Ltd
90 North Road
Lerwick
Shetland Islands
ZE1 0PQ
01595 693579
www.jamiesonandsmith.co.uk

Louisa Harding
See Debbie Bliss

Rowan Yarns
Green Lane Mill
Holmfirth HD9 2BR
01484 681881
www.knitrowan.com

Rowan Yarn Classics
Green Lane Mill
Holmfirth HD9 2BR
01484 681881
www.ryclassic.com

Twilley's
c/o Angel Yarns
Angel House
77 North Street
Portslade
East Sussex
BN41 1DZ
0870 766 6212
www.angelyarns.com